MADE IN America

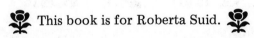 This book is for Roberta Suid.

MADE IN America

EIGHT GREAT ALL-AMERICAN CREATIONS

By Murray Suid and Ron Harris

▲
Addison-Wesley

Copyright © 1978 by Murray Suid and Ron Harris
All Rights Reserved
Addison-Wesley Publishing Company, Inc.
Reading, Massachusetts 01867
Printed in the United States of America

Book and jacket designed by Beth Anderson

Library of Congress Cataloging in Publication Data

Suid, Murray I
    Made in America.

    Includes index.
    SUMMARY: Discusses the rise of eight phenomena of
modern American culture: Coca-Cola, Superman, Monopoly,
King Kong, Levi's, Frisbees, Television, and McDonald's.
    1. Commercial products—United States—Juvenile
literature. 2. United States—Civilization—Juvenile
literature. [1 Commercial products] I. Harris, Ron,
1949-   joint author.   II. Title.

ISBN 0-201-07073-1-H
ISBN 0-201-07074-X-P
 BCDEFGHIJK-MA-79

The permissions listed under Credits on page 185 are an extension of this
copyright page.

Acknowledgments

We could never have done this book without the help of a great many friends, strangers, and corporations. They shared stories, answered questions, made suggestions, corrected our mistakes, loaned books, clipped articles from newspapers, provided photographs, and perhaps most important, gave us endless encouragement.

So thank you: Richard Adler, Fran Angelesco, Ralph Anspach, Sid Ascher, Judy Baxter, Steve Beck, Dave Brown, Bob Bryant, Jo Cahow, Peter Carroll, Ed Davis, Bob de Shaw, Toby Dills, Susan Drake, Bruce Dumont, Sue Dunlop, Maryanne Easley, Jean Eastman, Education Today Inc., Jack Ellis, Ken Eschman, Elma "Pem" Farnsworth, Mitch Farris, Barbara Ford, Mark Fryberger, Cliff Gardner, Mike Gold, Orville Goldner, Enid Goldstein, Judy Goodnow, Mark Goodnow, Sandy Goodnow, Warren Goodnow, John Hambrick, Jean Harper, Sol Harrison, Ted Haynes, Sandee Henry, Elizabeth Jochimen, Stancil Johnson, Deann Kato, Wyn Kato, KPIX-TV, KQED-TV, KRON-TV, Bette Krueger, Janet Lai, Bill Leikam, Blanche Lewis, Jamie Loftis, Greg Lyon, Richard McDonald, McDonald's Corp., Goldy Norton, Palo Alto Public Library, Parker Brothers, William Patterson, Mike Peak, Janet Pecha, Gloria Pitzer, Charles Pollock, Bruce Raskin, Elaine Ratner, Victoria Rouse, San Bernardino Public Library, San Bernardino Sun-Telegram, Leonard Sidlow, Jerry Siegel, Jack Stuart, Larry Suid, Roberta Suid, Harold Terhune, Don Thompson, Irwin Ungerleider, Whamo Manufacturing Inc., Burton Wolf, Leona Wong.

Contents

Introduction

Elizabeth Magie
Walt Morrison
Jerry Siegel and *Joe Shuster*
Merian Cooper, Ernest Schoedsack, Willis O'Brien
John Pemberton
Levi Strauss
Philo Farnsworth
Richard and *Maurice McDonald*

You may not know it but you are looking at a list of inventors who helped shape the way we live today. These are the unfamous people behind Monopoly, the Frisbee, Superman, King Kong, Coca-Cola, Levi's, and television.

You might not think of Monopoly or McDonald's as being inventions. But by the time you have read this book, you may agree that it takes as much imagination and persistence to invent a toy or a restaurant chain as it does to invent something like the light bulb.

But why devote a book to things like games and food? The reason is simple. Just as we can learn a lot about ancient peoples by studying their everyday objects such as arrowheads and pottery, we can get to know ourselves better by thinking about our own artifacts.

Along the way, you will have a chance to go behind the scenes, to find out how some of the familiar things in your life are made. A hundred years ago, this "tour" wouldn't have been necessary. People knew where their food, clothing and toys came from. If they wanted meat, they hunted for it or slaughtered livestock. Most meals were cooked at home. Clothes, too, were homemade, often using cloth that was homespun. The same is true for toys; these were usually made of natural materials—a dried-up apple for a doll's head, a nut shell and an acorn for a "ball and cup" toy.

How different it is today. We eat Big Macs but few of us know how they are put together (and fewer, still, like to think about the slaughterhouses the meat comes from). We quench our thirst with drinks made from "secret recipes." We buy toys created by highly-trained designers using plastic materials only scientists understand. And we get most of our entertainment from an electronic box that we control by pushing a button. How many of us know how it works?

There are so many mysteries. We will try to solve some of these in the pages ahead. You will see how denim fabric becomes a pair of Levi's and find out what makes cartoon characters move. You will follow the reporters and technicians as they put together the six o'clock news, and you will look over the shoulders of artists and writers as they create a comic book.

And you won't have to stand at the sidelines. We invite you to be a creator yourself. Many successful inventors believe that the best training for a would-be inventor is practice in solving problems. It's especially good to do activities that involve using one's hands—being handy. This is why we have included tips on how to make flip-books and animated movies, how to toss and catch a Frisbee, how to cook your own brand of burgers, how to produce radio and television programs, how to sew, how to draw comics, and how to make photo comics in case you do not like to draw. You'll even learn the secrets of calf roping and bull riding.

We hope the book helps you become more creative. We hope it tells you something about America. But most of all, we hope it gives you a lot of fun.

Murray Suid
Ron Harris

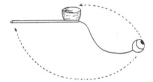

Superman

Almost everyone knows Superman, fighter for truth, justice and the American way. What most people do not know is that the Man of Steel was not born on the planet Krypton. He was born in Cleveland, Ohio, and his "parents" were two schoolboys.

Jerry Siegel and Joe Shuster were high school kids in Cleveland in 1933, at the worst part of the Great Depression. These were dark times for America. Money was scarce, millions were out of work, and despairing families waited in lines for bread and soup. If ever the country needed a hero, this was the time. One night, just such a hero—Superman—came to life in Jerry Siegel's mind.

Both Siegel and Shuster were rather ordinary kids who were shy and often bullied. They made up for this by living lives rich in fantasy. The boys were fans of science-fiction, which was still new in the 1930s. They listened to adventure stories on the radio and read the thrilling tales in the pulp magazines. The "pulps" were thick monthly magazines of short stories, and usually, one long story featuring a daring hero like Doc Savage, the Shadow or Operator 5. The magazines got their name from the cheap pulp paper on which they were printed. The pulps were a kind of forerunner to comic books, which in 1933 had not yet been invented.

The idea of Superman came to Jerry Siegel one night just before he fell asleep. All the stories and science-fiction adventures he had read seemed to come together in his head, and out of it all came the notion of a powerful champion of the downtrodden, who could bend the strongest steel and laugh at bullets.

Siegel spent most of the night scribbling down the first Superman story. The next morning, he showed the story to his friend Shuster, who was an aspiring artist. Shuster was caught up in Siegel's excitement and designed Superman's costume. The first Superman story, written by Siegel and illustrated by Shuster, appeared in a mimeographed science-fiction magazine put out by the pair.

Siegel and Shuster were convinced their creation was for bigger things than fan magazines. They decided to try for the "big time" by submitting Superman to the companies that produced newspaper comic strips. Time after time their strip was rejected. Some editors said the strip was crude and amateurish. Others said the character was stupid and totally unbelievable. All agreed that the public would never be interested in Superman.

For six years the pair kept at it, but still nobody wanted Superman. During those years, though, the comic book came into being. At first comic books were reprintings of popular newspaper strips, but after a while, new material began to appear. Comic book publishers wanted to produce the new magazines as cheaply as possible, and since child labor has always been cheap labor, many teen-agers found themselves working in the new medium. Among these were Jerry Siegel and Joe Shuster. The pair produced such strips as "Dr Occult" and "Slam Bradley." Most of their work appeared in *Detective Comics*, a title which is still being published today.

One day Siegel and Shuster heard that the editor of *Detective Comics* was looking for an action series to kick off his new magazine,

Jerry Siegel and Joe Shuster, creators of Superman

Action Comics. Eagerly, they presented Superman to the editor. The editor took one long look at the cover drawing, showing Superman lifting a car above his head, and said, "Nobody's going to believe this!" Still, something about the character appealed to the editor, and Siegel and Shuster were offered $130 for all rights to Superman, forever.

At that time, $130 was a lot of money, when a loaf of bread cost 15 cents and the movies a dime. The boys were thrilled when they signed the contract but they would regret this decision for the rest of their lives.

Superman was an instant success. The first issues of *Action* sold out. Something about the character appealed to everybody, and the public began clamoring for more, more and still more. Superman got a magazine all his own, then a radio series, an animated cartoon series, newspaper strip and a movie serial. Siegel and Shuster had to hire assistants to keep up with

A 1934 advertisement that appeared in a pulp magazine. Doc Savage was a crime fighter of tremendous strength and intelligence who resembled the early Superman in many ways.

A typical pulp magazine. Pulps featured stories of action, science fiction and fantastic adventure.

the work load. The comics company, now called DC Comics, was making millions.

Siegel and Shuster realized they had sold the rights to a gold mine. Time and again they sued the comics company, demanding a cut of the growing Superman empire. Several times they did get more money; by 1940 one magazine reported they were making $75,000 a year. But they never received the percentage they wanted. Then World War II called Jerry Siegel to battle. After the war Siegel returned to DC. He wrote Superman on and off for some twenty years.

During the "off" periods he battled DC unsuccessfully in court.

By the late 1960s Siegel and Shuster faded into obscurity. Siegel tried to create other characters. He had some success with Superboy, but basically he was a one-idea man. All his other creations flopped. Shuster did work for several comics companies until his eyesight began to fail, and he had to retire. Superman rolled on, becoming a TV series in 1951 and finding huge audiences throughout the world. In 1965, the Man of Steel appeared in a Broadway play

One of Joe Shuster's earliest drawings of the new hero. "The Superman," as he was called, wore tights and an undershirt instead of the red-and-blue costume.

called *It's a Bird It's a Plane It's Superman.* Everyone knew Superman, but nobody remembered Siegel and Shuster.

Then, in 1973, came the news that Superman was going to appear in a big feature movie. The producer paid DC Comics $3 million for the right to make the film. Jerry Siegel, now old and broke, saw one more chance to make something off his old character. This time instead of going to the courts, he went to the newspapers and television. He told a story of how he and Joe Shuster had been destroyed by DC Comics, saying that Superman, the American dream, had brought them an "American nightmare." The American public, with its classic love for the underdog, took the story to its heart. Soon Siegel's and Shuster's names appeared in newspapers around the country. The people at DC Comics were worried. Even though they legally owed Siegel and Shuster nothing, they knew the growing bad publicity could spell disaster for the super-expensive (and hopefully super-profitable) Superman movie. The company responded to public pressure.

Just before Christmas of 1975, DC Comics and Siegel and Shuster reached a financial agreement. Also their names, long absent from the comic pages, appeared as the creators of Superman, the world's first and mightiest superhero. With fame undimmed, the Man of Steel flew into the 1970s.

Superman Through the Years

The first Superman was very different from the Superman we know today. He wore a red-and-blue costume with an S on the front, but he was a much weaker person. At first, Superman could not fly. Instead, he leaped great distances. While bullets did not hurt him, an artillery shell could break his skin. He did not have X-ray vision.

Clark Kent, Superman's alter ego, was a newspaper reporter right from the start. Joe Shuster, who worked for his school newspaper, suggested the reporter disguise. Clark's name came from two movie actors, Clark Gable and Kent Taylor. Lois Lane, Kent's fellow reporter, was named after Lois Amster, a girl Shuster secretly admired.

As the Superman comic continued, Siegel quickly discovered that the readers liked Superman's *superness*. The Man of Steel became stronger. Now he could fly. His X-ray vision could penetrate anything except lead and people's clothing. Bombs no longer hurt him.

A page from the first Superman story in *Action Comics* #1.

In the 1940s Superman starred in a newspaper strip.

In 1941 Superman first appeared on film in a series of cartoons. Then the Man of Steel appeared in serials, starting in 1948, and won a television series in 1951. Kirk Alyn played the movie Superman; George Reeves wore the famous "S" on television.

THE SUPERMAN FAMILY

GUIDE TO CHARACTERS IN SUPERMAN FAMILY PORTRAIT

A. **SUPERMAN**

B. **SUPERGIRL** . . . . COUSIN TO SUPERMAN . . . NOW APPEARING IN HER OWN MAGAZINE.

C. **JIMMY OLSEN** . . . SUPERMAN'S PAL . . . APPEARS IN HIS OWN MAGAZINE.

D. **LUCY LANE** . . . GIRL FRIEND OF JIMMY OLSEN . . . SISTER TO LOIS LANE.

E. **PERRY WHITE** . . . EDITOR OF DAILY PLANET.

F. **LOIS LANE** . . . SUPERMAN'S GIRL FRIEND . . . APPEARS IN HER OWN MAGAZINE.

G. **LANA LANG** . . . LOIS LANE'S COMPETITOR FOR SUPERMAN'S ATTENTION . . . WAS SUPERMAN'S GIRL FRIEND WHEN HE WAS SUPERBOY.

H. **MARTHA AND JONATHAN KENT** . . . SUPERMAN'S ADOPTED PARENTS WHEN HE FIRST ARRIVED ON EARTH.

I. **KRYPTO** . . . SUPERBOY'S PET.

J. **STREAKY** . . . SUPERGIRL'S PET.

K. **COMET** . . . ANOTHER OF SUPERGIRL'S PETS.

L. **MR. MXYZPTLK** . . . A NEMESIS OF SUPERMAN, WHO CAN ONLY BE THWARTED BY HAVING HIM REPEAT HIS NAME BACKWARDS (KLTPZYXM).

M. **LEGION OF SUPER-HEROES** . . . A GROUP OF CRIME-FIGHTERS IN THE 30th CENTURY OF WHICH SUPERBOY IS A MEMBER.

N. **LARA AND JOR-EL** . . . SUPERMAN'S REAL PARENTS FROM THE PLANET KRYPTON.

O. **BIZARRO SUPERMAN** . . . A SUPERMAN FROM A WORLD EXACTLY OPPOSITE THIS ONE. FOR EXAMPLE . . . THE WORLD IS SQUARE, NOT ROUND. UGLINESS IS BEAUTIFUL. etc.

P. **PROFESSOR POTTER** . . . A FRIEND OF JIMMY OLSEN, WHOSE FORMULAS GIVE JIMMY THE OPPORTUNITY TO CHANGE SHAPES AND GO TO DIFFERENT TIME PERIODS.

Q. **LORI LEMARIS** . . . ANOTHER FORMER GIRLFRIEND OF SUPERMAN'S

The Superman family

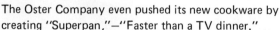

FASTER THAN A TV DINNER - MIGHTIER THAN A TAKE-OUT ORDER...
ABLE TO CREATE MAGNIFICENT MEALS AT A SINGLE BOUND,
SUPER PAN PITS SUPER VERSATILITY AGAINST THE FORCES OF
MEALTIME MONOTONY - ON THE SIDE OF THE AMERICAN HOME-
MAKER! A MASTER OF DISGUISE, SUPER PAN MAY APPEAR AS AN
ORDINARY CASSEROLE, BUT IN THE TWINKLING OF AN EYE CAN
CHANGE INTO A FONDUE POT, A TEMPURA COOKER, A CHAFING
DISH OR HANDSOME BUFFET SERVER! NO WONDER SUPER PAN
IS KNOWN TO GRATEFUL HOUSEWIVES FROM COAST TO COAST AS
THE NEMESIS OF BOREDOM!
NOW— FOLLOW SUPER PAN'S EXPLOITS IN THESE
EXCITING ADVENTURES

The Oster Company even pushed its new cookware by creating "Superpan,"—"Faster than a TV dinner."

Superman has become so well-known that many people make references to him in pictures and books. This is from the annual report of Palo Alto, California, which promoted itself as "Super-city."

Before long the other extreme was reached. Superman became *so* super that it was hard to write stories about him! It didn't seem fair to put a bunch of puny gangsters with machine guns against a man who could move mountains with his bare hands. There had to be a way to cut Superman down to size.

Siegel found the right gimmick in Kryptonite, the drifting chunks of Superman's dead home planet. Kryptonite robbed Superman of his strength and made him vulnerable again. Kryptonite breathed new life into a thousand old plots by stealing some of Superman's godlike powers. Kryptonite was used so often by idea-hungry writers that readers wondered if somebody was not hauling the stuff to earth by the truckload.

Even Kryptonite wore thin after a few years. Writers decided to liven up the series by creating new characters. Superman became something of a clown, fighting the likes of Mr. Mxyzptlk, a fifth-dimensional elf who drove Superman crazy with his dangerous antics. The Bizarros, a race of alien crea-

tures who were fascinated by Superman, appeared throughout the 1960s. The Bizarros had chalk-white bodies that looked like rock, and they spoke in baby-talk. There were Bizarro equivalents of Superman, Clark Kent and Lois Lane. After a while, the Bizarros even got their own series.

New characters were also added to the super-side of the family. The Superboy series told of the Man of Steel's adventures as a kid. Other stories told of the feats of Superbaby. Supergirl, Superman's cousin from Krypton, landed on Earth in the future and met Superman when he crashed through the time barrier. Then came the super-pets. Superboy found Krypto, the super-dog, for a companion. Hot on Krypto's heels followed a super-horse, a super-cat, and even a super-monkey. Things were getting a bit out of hand.

Superman went through a major overhaul in the early 1970s. Deciding that the Man of Steel had become old-fashioned, the writers and artists had him exchange his old newspaper post for a job as a TV newsman. Clark Kent wore his hair longer and dressed in more stylish clothes. Kryptonite was destroyed. No obstacles remained in Superman's path, but by this time his petty-crook-fighting days were over. The villains Superman fought were usually as powerful as the Man of Steel himself.

Recently, Superman has starred in a series of large-sized comic books in which he has met such heroes as Spider-Man, Wonder Woman and Muhammad Ali. After nearly forty years, the Man of Steel is still going strong, and there is no end in sight.

How Superman Flies

It is not hard to make impossible things happen in cartoons and comics, but when it came to making actor George Reeves "fly" for the Superman TV series, the television people had a problem on their hands.

At first, they used small wires to support the actor in front of a blank movie screen. The wires were attached to a harness under Superman's costume and were so thin the camera could not pick them up. When Superman was supposed to fly, a movie of scenery flashing by was projected onto the screen from behind. However, the wires were not very strong, and one time they broke. Reeves fell to the floor and was nearly hurt. After that accident, the TV people built a strong boom from which Superman dangled. The boom was kept out of sight of the camera. It could be moved up and down or in a circle to make it seem as if Superman was flying.

For take-offs, Reeves would bounce on a hidden trampoline and leap into the air. When the *take-off* was spliced together with a *flying* scene, it looked as if Superman had really flown up into the sky. Landings were done much the same way, but this time a ladder was set up out of sight of the camera. The actor would jump off the ladder into the picture, seemingly dropping out of the sky. One familiar scene to TV Superman fans is the one in which Reeves flies out of a window. To do this, the actor leaped through a phony window on the movie set onto a pile of mattresses on the other side. All the camera could see was Superman leaping out the window; he appeared to be flying off—up, up and away.

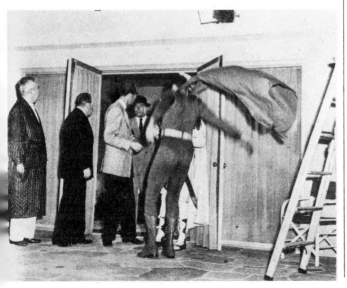

The History of Comics

The art of telling stories with pictures goes all the way back to prehistory. Cave people often recorded their hunts in pictures on the walls of their homes. Later, civilizations like the Egyptians used drawings in sequences to tell of the deeds of their rulers. But none of these were really comics.

Comics, as we know them, began a few hundred years ago when French and English artists invented the cartoon—a single picture or *panel* which included dialogue in the scene. Cartoonists of the day usually poked fun at life and politics. The cartoon tradition carried over to the United States, where the ever-inventive Benjamin Franklin came up with the *balloon* to contain dialogue and indicate the speaker. Gradually cartoonists began telling their stories with more than one picture. Finally, in the early 1900s, American newspapers ran the first true comic strips. The new art form caught on, and the number of strips grew quickly.

The first newspaper strips told jokes and funny stories, but in the late 1920s some writers turned to stories of high adventure. Science fiction strips like "Buck Rogers" and aviation strips like "Tailspin Tommy" were very popular. These early adventure strips were still drawn in a cartoon style. Then, in the early 1930s, three men—Harold Foster in his "Tarzan" strip and

Storytelling with pictures is as old as the cave dwellers. Eventually, words and pictures combined to tell the story. In the eleventh century, the Bayeux Tapestry told the story of William the Conqueror in labeled pictures.

This cartoon strip excerpt from 1784 was drawn by Thomas Rowlandson, an English satirist. The strip shows an early use of dialogue balloons.

"Buster Brown" was one of ▶ the many humor strips run by American newspapers in the 1910s and 1920s. The cartoonlike drawings and funny stories gave the strips the name "comic strips" or "funny papers."

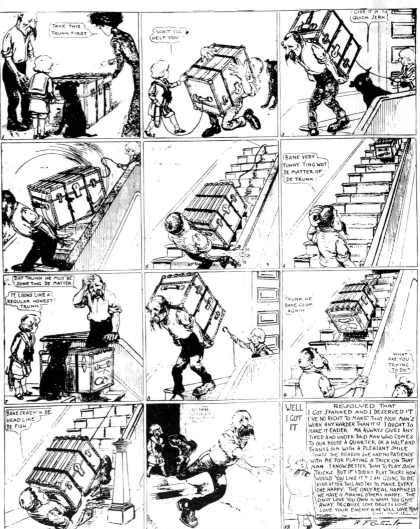

The name "comics" stuck even after the strips stopped being comic. These panels are from "Scorchy Smith" and "Terry and the Pirates." The artists, Noel Sickles and Milton Caniff, developed the realistic drawing style that influenced early comics.

Funnies on Parade, published in 1929, was probably the first comic book. It reprinted newspaper comics. Not until several years later did all-new stories begin to appear in comic books.

Before the superheroes, comics featured stories about cowboys, detectives and pirates.

Jack Kirby helped create Captain America in 1940. His new style of superhero drawing is still influencing artists today.

Noel Sickles and Milton Caniff in "Scorchy Smith" and "Terry and the Pirates"—invented more realistic styles which changed the look of all adventure strips to come.

When comic books began in the mid-1930s, the writers and artists were strongly influenced by these strips. Many of the artists were young and unskilled, and many imitated or copied outright (or as cartoonists say, "swiped") the work of men like Foster and Caniff. Caniff was an especially strong influence on many young comic artists, including Joe Shuster.

Slowly comic books developed their own styles and traditions. Comic book stories and artwork became less and less like newspaper strips. Jack Kirby, an artist who helped create Captain America in the 1940s and is still working in comics, created a whole new comic-book style based on muscular figures, dynamic action and huge machines. Kirby's influence was so great that it is seen even in the artwork of that earliest of all superheroes, Superman.

Comics in Other Lands

We are so used to looking at American comics that it is easy to forget how widespread comic books really are. Comics may have been invented in America, but they are far more popular abroad than they are in their native land.

The familiar American comic book—the monthly with from 32 to 80 pages in color—is found almost nowhere else in the world. These comics from Italy and France are the same size and are printed on the same paper as magazines such as *People*. The magazines appear once a week. Each issue contains parts of several serialized adventure stories. The stories run 3 to 8 pages a week until they end. Most run about 48 pages in all. Each issue also carries several short cartoon strips. European comics magazines do not carry just comics. In each magazine are articles about sports heroes, rock singers and movie stars, as well as news of fan clubs and pen-pal pages.

Another form of comics common in Europe is the *album*. The serialized strips which appear in weekly comics magazines are collected into

hardbound or paperbound books selling for from $2 to $12.

Not all European comics are for kids. Many albums, like the bottom one in the picture above, are intended for adult readers. Many educated people in Europe look down on comics just as some people do in America. However, thousands of European adults, educated and uneducated alike, read comics.

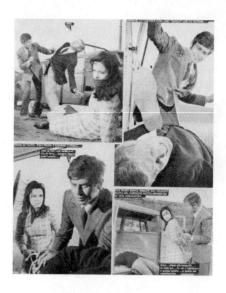

A popular type of adult comic in Italy, Mexico and several other countries is the photo-novel. Instead of using drawings, the photo-novel tells its stories with photographs. Photo-novels usually depict love stories or mysteries. In Mexico, some soap-opera photo-comics have sold a million copies an issue.

Photo-comics are a fun way to make comics without drawing. See how to make your own on pages 30–33.

The number of comics fans in Europe is so big that American fans find it hard to believe. A great many European fans are adults. They publish *fanzines*, like *Sgt. Kirk* above, devoted to the study of comics history and to show-casing new talent. Many Italian comics fans are also crazy about newspaper adventure strips. This "Rip Kirby" book is one of hundreds of Italian magazines which reprint strips all but forgotten in the United States. The Italian strip fans start with a strip's first appearance and print every single strip, which means that some reprint series run over *40 volumes* at $4 to $6 each. Yet strip fanciers pay this and cry for more.

It is interesting that except for translations of American comic books (which are not that popular), there are no superheroes in Europe. The closest Europe comes to America's familiar costumed hero is the Phantom—actually an old American newspaper hero, nearly forgotten at home but one of Europe's most popular characters. Europe's favorite comics subjects include exotic adventures, detectives, spies, westerns and science-fiction.

Enthusiasm for comics in Europe is nothing compared to that of Japan. Every week comics for kids and adults alike flood the newsstands.

Comics for kids are thick (up to 300 pages), cheaply printed magazines with a few color pages on the front. Remaining pages are printed in colored ink on different colored paper: black on orange, purple on white, black on green. Each issue carries, in addition to short cartoon strips, 7 or 8 serialized adventure stories. Each chapter runs 30 pages or more; a complete story may last 600 pages.

Japanese comics are not only the biggest comics in the world, they are among the most violent—to the dismay of many Japanese parents. Just about any subject with lots of action is fair game for Japanese comic strips.

Superheroes are very popular in Japan. Most are variations on giant robots and monster-fighters, which are also the most common subjects on Japanese kids' TV shows. But the comics have stories about everything from cowboys to detectives, from ghosts to samurai. One particular Japanese craze is the sports hero. Every kids' comic has at least one heroic baseball player, not to mention heroic race car drivers, martial arts champions, boxers, wrestlers, swimmers, runners and, in one case, even heroic bowlers!

How a Comic is Made

Every month, dozens of comic books hit the stands. In a year companies like Marvel or DC Comics may publish thousands of pages of story. Writing and drawing so many comics takes a lot of time, and time is precious in the comics industry. In order to speed production and keep things running smoothly, comics companies have developed a sort of comic book assembly line. Here's how it works.

The comic begins with the writer. After consulting with an editor, the writer comes up with an idea for the next issue's story. From here the writer may go one of two ways. Write a *script* like this one. The script describes panel by panel what will appear in the comic. Other times the writer will only write a *synopsis*, a short summary of what happens in the story. Then the artist breaks the story down into panels. The writer provides the actual dialogue and captions based on the completed drawings.

The script method gives the writer the biggest say in telling the story in pictures. It is used mostly by companies like DC Comics, Gold Key and Archie. The synopsis method gives the artist more freedom in the storytelling, but takes some away from the writer. It is used mostly by Marvel Comics, which invented the technique.

PAGE 15 (4 panels)

PANEL 1. Looking from inside the Tyranean ship, the
          STARSHADOW is heading straight for the viewport.
          Arloc and lieutenant react.

          ARLOC: It...it's not stopping! They're going
                  to RAM us!!

PANEL 2. Lance and Val start to move from their position
          against the wall.

          LANCE (Thinx): Karel is giving us just the
                          distraction we NEED!

          LANCE (Aloud): Come on, Val, let's MOVE!

PANEL 3. LS Arloc and lieutenant spin around as Val and
          Lance come charging toward them.

          ARLOC: Wha--you've ESCAPED! But those chains
                  were solid ADAMANTUM!

          VAL: Even adamantum can be cut with a concealed
                  WRIST BLASTER, Arloc! We were just waiting
                  for the right MOMENT...

          VAL: ...And this is IT!

PANEL 4. Val grabs Arloc's arm as he tries to pull a gun.

          ARLOC: FOOLS! You waited too LONG! In another
                  moment that ship will COLLIDE with us...
                  and we'll ALL be dead!

          VAL: Don't COUNT on it, Commander!

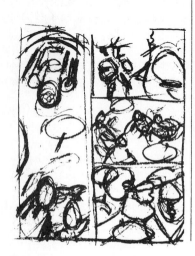

The *penciller* converts the script or synopsis into drawings, usually starting with rough sketches like these. The sketches help the penciller decide what size and shape the panels should be and how the drawings will be composed.

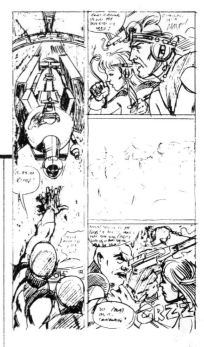

Sometimes more sketches may be needed to establish the look of villains and secondary characters.

The page is usually drawn "one and a half up," which means one and a half times the size of the printed comic. The larger size is easier for the artist to work with, and when the printer reduces it, the finished art looks crisper than if it had been drawn "same size."

Comic pages are drawn on sheets of heavy paper called *bristol board.* First the penciller "roughs in" the figures, leaving space for the dialogue balloons. (In the strip to the right, the third panel is still in a rough stage.) The artist then "tightens the pencils" to come up with a finished drawing.

The pencilled page is given to the *letterer.* The letterer rules the panel borders in ink, then draws pencil *guide lines* to keep the lettering straight.

Working from the script, the letterer inks in the dialogue, captions and sound effects, and draws the balloons. The letterer uses pens of different weights to make regular and bold letters. The first three panels on the right are lettered and the fourth is just started.

The printing process used for comics cannot reproduce pencil drawings. The pencils must be gone over in black ink. This is called *inking.* Using a brush and pen, the inker *renders* the penciller's drawings in black and white. Occasionally the pen-

ciller will ink his own work. However comics producers have found work usually goes faster if a penciller does nothing but pencil and an inker nothing but ink.

Inking is important to the final look of a comic page. No two people draw exactly alike, and the inker's drawing style almost always changes the pencil artist's work somewhat. Many pencillers draw in outline, leaving things like shadows up to the inker. Others pencil everything the way they want it to look when inked. At left, only one panel is not inked.

At the top is a pencil drawing and how it looked when inked by two different inkers. You can see what a great difference an inker can make.

If the artwork is to be printed in a black-and-white comic, it's now ready for the printer. If it is to be in color, another step remains.

Most people think the original art for comics is colored in. This is not so. The drawings stay in black and white. A copy is made of each finished page, reduced to comic-book size. Then an artist called the *colorist* paints the reduced copy with watercolors, indicating how the printed page should look. The original art and the colored copies are sent to the printer.

If you have looked closely at a color comic, you will see that the colors are made up of combinations of dots or solid areas of red, yellow, and blue. The printer's *color separators* decide which areas should be printed in which combinations to give the colors specified by the colorist. From their *separations* the printer prepares four sets of printing plates: black, red, yellow and blue.

The comics are printed on huge printing presses capable of printing many thousands of copies an hour. The presses fold, staple and trim the books as well. Out the other end comes a finished comic!

A Comic Dictionary

Comics writers and artists have a language all their own to describe the elements of a comic page. Here are a few terms you will want to know if you would like to speak "comicese."

Comics are told using pictures called *panels*, each of which is outlined by the *panel border*. The space between panels, as well as the white space between the pages where the comic is stapled, is called the *gutter*.

Often the writer will give information to the reader in the form of a *caption* (1). The words in the caption are called the *narration*.

The words spoken by the characters in the story are called the *dialogue*. Dialogue is contained in *dialogue balloons* (or simply "balloons") with *pointers* indicating who is speaking (2). A character's thoughts appear in a *thought balloon* (3). Thought balloons are usually shaped like clouds. Instead of a pointer, the thought balloon has a string of *bubbles* pointing toward the thinker. Words that are shouted or spoken very dramatically are sometimes put in *splash balloons* (4), which are shaped like little explosions.

In everyday life, the meaning of the words a person speaks depends a lot on which words the speaker emphasizes. Comic writers try to imitate patterns of speech by using *boldface lettering* to show which words a character is emphasizing. Sometimes the hero's name is put in boldface each time it appears. This is an old tradition which started as a way to make superheroes even more dramatic. It is seldom done any more.

Another old comic tradition is that of ending every sentence with an exclamation point instead of a period. This tradition began in the early days of comics, when the cheap printing would often be unable to reproduce little dots like periods. If an exclamation point were used, even if the dot disappeared, the vertical line would still be there to show where the sentence ended. Besides, exclamation points added excitement and urgency to the dialogue, and the gimmick remained in use long after printing improved.

The other often-seen comic tool is the *sound effect* (5). Comic writers often dream up imaginative words to describe the sound of a ray gun, an explosion, a blow or a crash. Sound effects are usually lettered in outline or *open lettering*, so that color may be added.

Some other helpful comic terms include *splash panel* (the single large panel which opens a story, sometimes presenting an event which appears later in the strip); *spread* (the two pages you see when you open a comic), and *wraparound cover* (a drawing which begins on the front cover of a comic and extends around onto the back cover).

How to Collect Comics

No. 1   JUNE, 1938

Action Comics #1, containing the first appearance of Superman.

Comic collecting is a hobby that appeals to young and old alike. Since the early 1960s, comics "fandom", as collectors call it, has grown to include thousands of members.

Most comic collectors begin by buying the current issues of their favorite comics. Soon, they start seeking out back issues, trying to complete "runs" (all the issues of a given comic). This activity often leads them to collect other titles, and then others. A collector might trade comics with other collectors or buy issues from one of the country's many comics dealers.

Fans collect comics for many reasons. Some simply like a certain comic hero and collect all the books in which that character appears. Others are fans of a particular artist. They try to find all the comics for which that artist has drawn. Serious art collectors often find it rough going, since until recently, few comics companies ever credited their artists and writers. Collectors may have to decide for themselves just who drew a particular story.

Some fans collect all the comics published by one company. Others specialize in the "Golden Age," which is the name given the early days of comics from 1935 to 1945. Other collectors are in it for the money, buying and reselling valuable comics.

Making money from comics is a recent invention. Over the last 10 years comics speculators have almost taken over the field, and rare comics now sell for prices that once would have made fans laugh.

One of the most valuable comics is *Action Comics #1*, the first appearance of Superman. While it wasn't the first comic by any means,

Issue 52 of *X-Men*, at left, sells for less than $1. The very next issue sells for 6 times as much. What's the difference? Issue 53 was drawn by Barry Smith, whom art fans consider "highly collectible."

Action #1 was such an important event in comics history that many collectors want a copy. There are not many to be found. During World War II, thousands of comic books were turned in for recycling, so all the "Golden Age" titles are scarce. Depending on who is selling it, *Action #1* may cost from $2000 to $8000.

More recent comics are worth money, too, but the prices are much lower. Fan interest has a lot to do with how much a comic sells for. Marvel comics are presently the most popular, and the first issue of titles like *Fantastic Four* and *Spider-Man* sell for upwards of $300. Occasionally, a comic will become a surprise hit and will jump in value almost overnight. Marvel's *Conan #1* (1970) and *Howard the Duck #1* (1976) were selling for $5 to $10 apiece within months of their release. However, speculators cannot always predict the trends. Many would-be millionaires have wound up with hundreds of copies of a comic they were sure would be a hit—but instead was a flop.

First issues of popular comics are especially prized by collectors.

The trouble with comics money-making is that with all the bally-hoo about valuable comics, people get the idea that *all* comics are valuable. Someone will put out a stack of comics collected over the last two years and expect to cart it to a comic store and get $1 for each. In fact, few recent comics are particularly valuable. Most titles sell for less than 50¢ for several years before finally rising in value. Other comics, especially those from unpopular companies like Charlton and Gold Key, almost never go up much in value. Westerns, romance comics and war stories are also usually bad investments.

As widespread as comics money-making is, there are hundreds of fans who are not out to make a quick buck. These fans are more interested in the whole world of comics. Many comics fans publish "fanzines," home-made comics fan magazines. Would-be comic artists and writers put out fanzines with their own comic strips and stories. Other fans write articles about current comics. Still others take a serious historical interest in comics and publish the results of their research into comics history and comics personnel.

Comics which are missing their covers or otherwise damaged bring very low prices. However, many art and story fans will buy damaged copies to read when they cannot afford the high price of a perfect copy.

Many major cities have comics conventions each year. A convention often centers around the "dealers' room" where comics sellers peddle their wares. The convention usually has a program of events, including talks by comic artists and writers, art shows, costume contests and movies. Conventions are a great place to meet other fans, as well as to find back issues which are hard to come by in your hometown.

The growing popularity of comics fandom has brought about the opening of comics shops in cities all over America. These stores sell old and new comics, posters, books and comics-related items. Comics shops are another good place to meet fellow fans.

Here are just three of the dozens of fanzines published by comic book fans. It's hard to find back issues—or even "current" fanzines—because of small print runs. Few fanzines last more than an issue or two, because they make no money for the publisher.

How to Get into Comics Fandom

The Buyer's Guide for Comics Fandom (Dynapubs Enterprises, 15800 Route 84 North, East Moline, IL 61244) is a weekly newspaper for comics advertising. Each issue is made up mostly of ads from fans and dealers selling comics, books, posters, artwork and the like. Every other issue has a large section devoted to articles and news about comics. Many fans use the *Buyer's Guide* to buy comic material or to find the names of other fans. Each issue of TBG usually has several ads from fanzine publishers looking for contributors. A sample issue of TBG costs $1; a subscription (52 issues) is $10 per year.

The Comic Reader (Street Enterprises, Box 255, Menomonee Falls, WI 53051) is a "newszine," a small monthly fanzine which prints news about what is going on in bigtime comics. A typical issue lists the contents, artists and writers of all the new comics to be issued the next month, as well as bulletins about behind-the-scenes activities at the comics companies. Other features include letters, interviews, TV and movie news, and a pocket checklist of new titles to refer to while shopping. Sample issues are 75¢; a year's subscription costs $7.00.

And don't forget to check your neighborhood for comics conventions and comics shops. Conventions are often so big a new fan might feel overwhelmed. But at shops, fans are always standing around swapping opinions and talking comics; you are likely to find others who share your interests.

How to Draw Comics

(31) FLYING SAUCER This drawing is started by drawing first the glass or plastic dome. Around the base of the dome, using the same foreshortened circles as on the round wedding cake, draw the platform. The body of the saucer is shallow. Notice that the far leg does not come down as far as the two near legs. Add the radar dish.

(32) SIMPLE CHAIR This exercise is started with a foreshortened square with a thickness on it. The two outside legs are drawn first and are the same length. The near leg is drawn longer than the first two and the peek-a-boo leg is drawn shorter. The back rest is drawn up vertically from the right side and is about the same thickness as the legs. Shade.

(33) SQUARE WEDDING CAKE This is started by drawing a small cube. Straight out from the two outside lower corners, draw two more dots. Make another dot just this side of the near corner. Complete as much of the foreshortened circle as would show. Complete this layer of the cake and draw the bottom part.

(34) WOODEN BUCKET A double foreshortened circle is used here. A dot in the center of the foreshortened circles is used to point the cracks along the top edge of the bucket. Notice the shading from dark to light and how the shading jumps to the right on the inside of the bucket.

(35) THE THICK LETTER "L" IN DIRECTION ONE The face of the "L" should be drawn first. All of the lines on the face go in only two different directions — vertical or direction one. After the face of the "L" is completed, draw the little short thickness lines in direction seven. It is important that they are all in direction and that they are the same length. Then connect the thickness lines and shade the left edge only.

(36) THE SIMPLE HOUSE FACING RIGHT Remember the thickness on windows should always be on the side farthest from you. The thickness is on the left in this drawing. Try to draw the walk from the door so that it does not appear to slant down hill. A line extended from the bottom edge of the shady side of the house can be used to check whether or not the walk goes down hill.

Are you itching to draw your own comics, but frustrated because you "can't even draw a straight line"? Maybe it will cheer you up to know that even professional artists very seldom can draw a straight line—that's what rulers are for!

However, if you want to start learning how to draw better, here are some books to look at. The first three will help you to make things "look like they should." The fourth talks about the mechanics of writing and drawing comics.

Remember, though, that the only way really to learn to draw is to practice. Use the books to start out, then draw, draw, draw!

Drawing Textbook by Bruce McIntyre (Audio-Visual Drawing Program, 1014 N. Wright Street, Santa Ana, California, 1971)—$1.00 (See page left.)

Drawing Textbook is the dull name given to an exciting little booklet for the person who is a beginner at the art of drawing. Bruce McIntyre, once an animator for the Walt Disney Studios, says that most people cannot draw simply because everyone has convinced them they cannot. Everybody, Mc-

Now we try again. If your shapes do not match mine it doesn't matter.

Any shape will do. Get the working principle. Remember the sides of the face should match. Do not make one cheek or ear larger than the other.

All blue lines are light lines. When drawn in as you want them, erase until faint, and then "bang in" the heavy lines for the final drawing.

Draw fairly large. Since your shapes are your own, you "originate" faces.

Intyre complains, mixes up *drawing*, which is as natural and easy as handwriting, with *art*, which is the work of geniuses like Leonardo da Vinci. People assume they have to be artists in order to draw.

Not so, says Bruce McIntyre, as he provides a series of simple exercises designed to teach ordinary, everyday people how to "talk" with a pencil. His lessons take the form of little exercise drawings, each a little harder than the one before. By drawing rockets, books, houses and rowboats, you can master the seven basic laws that will help make your drawings look "real."

Fun With A Pencil by Andrew Loomis (Viking Press, New York, 21st printing, 1977)—$10.95.

Andrew Loomis was a talented illustrator who worked from the 1920s through the 1950s. All his life he loved to draw people. In 1939, he wrote *Fun With A Pencil*, the first in a series of books on drawing. His aim was to get others to share in the fun of drawing for pleasure and for profit.

Though the text of the book is written for adults, aspiring cartoonists of all ages will find plenty of help to start them drawing. Loomis begins with "potato head" caricatures like those above (proving that no matter how badly you draw a circle, you can still make a funny face). Then he takes you through putting character into faces, making stick figures, drawing action and understanding perspective.

The only drawback of the book (other than its price—check it out from the library) is that Loomis moves rather fast in the last half. There is a lot of information packed into these 120 pages. Unlike McIntyre's *Drawing Textbook*, *Fun With A Pencil* is not the sort of book you can work through in a few days. But if you stick with it, you will not only have a lot of fun, you will also end up drawing some pretty good cartoons.

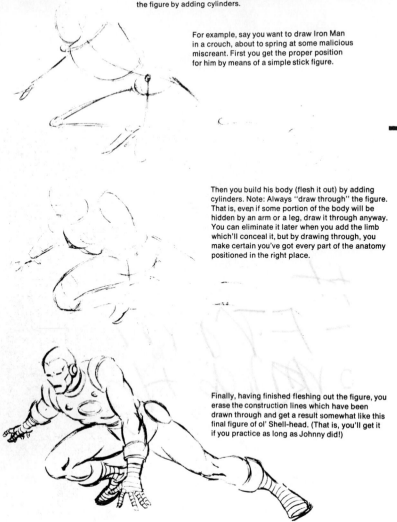

Notice how you can add ovals for the rib cage and the hips. Then, for the arms and legs, you can start building the figure by adding cylinders.

For example, say you want to draw Iron Man in a crouch, about to spring at some malicious miscreant. First you get the proper position for him by means of a simple stick figure.

Then you build his body (flesh it out) by adding cylinders. Note: Always "draw through" the figure. That is, even if some portion of the body will be hidden by an arm or a leg, draw it through anyway. You can eliminate it later when you add the limb which'll conceal it, but by drawing through, you make certain you've got every part of the anatomy positioned in the right place.

Finally, having finished fleshing out the figure, you erase the construction lines which have been drawn through and get a result somewhat like this final figure of ol' Shell-head. (That is, you'll get it if you practice as long as Johnny did!)

How To Draw Comics The Marvel Way by Stan Lee and John Buscema. (Simon & Schuster, New York, 1978)— $8.95.

The drawing of superheroes is a specialized art all by itself. Lots of action, lots of drama, lots of muscles—those are the rules. In this book, *Marvel Comics* publisher Stan Lee teams up with illustrator John Buscema (bew-SEMM-uh) to teach you how to draw superheroes in the style that made *Marvel* famous.

Though Lee's name is first on the credits, his contribution is limited to a few bad jokes. The book really belongs to John Buscema. Buscema, one of the most gifted of American comics artists, talks about constructing heroic figures, drawing faces, laying out stories and finishing drawings. He deals with such little-known phases of comic art as balancing light and dark areas and composing panels for maximum drama. For the amateur comic artist who is serious about someday "cracking the big time," this is an excellent textbook.

The big drawback of *How To Draw Comics The Marvel Way* is that it is too professionally-oriented for the casual or beginning artist. Buscema tries to start at the very beginning, but he still assumes you can already at least draw good figures. The beginner is likely to become badly frustrated when he follows all the steps yet does not get one of Buscema's lean, graceful drawings. The fact is, those drawings also contain years of study and anatomy practice which are not mentioned in the text. Buscema is so good that he makes it look easy to turn a stick figure into a dynamic hero. But you may want to put a good dose of McIntyre and Loomis under your belt before you do more than look at the pretty pictures.

Make Your Own Comics For Fun And Profit by Richard Cummings (Henry Walck, Inc., New York, 1976)—$8.95.

Unlike the last three books, *Make Your Own Comics* does not tell you how to draw. Instead, author Cummings concentrates on how to tell stories with comics and cartoons. His chapters talk about how to get ideas; developing a personal style; using "comics shorthand" like speed lines, stars and cuss marks; putting a story idea into panels and rendering your drawings. He even has a chapter about ways to reproduce your strips, from hectograph to offset printing. The book is heavily illustrated with examples of comic strips drawn by kids, with a few pages by professionals thrown in.

Cummings offers many useful ideas and insights, such as when he talks about how to "pace" your stories and compose your panels. The

Jacket illustration from *Make Your Own Comics for Fun and Profit* by Richard Cummings.

chapter on reproduction, especially, is worth its weight in gold if you want to take your strips beyond the simple pencil-and-paper stage. However, the book is a bit thin, and a lot of space is taken up with other people's work. This makes it a bit expensive for what the book offers. You may want to hunt this one up at the library, too.

YOU CAN MAKE YOUR OWN COMICS

...WITHOUT DRAWING A THING!

© 1978 RON HARRIS & MURRAY SUID

IT'S FUN TO MAKE YOUR OWN COMICS...

...BUT NOT IF YOU DON'T LIKE WHAT YOU DRAW!

WELL, HERE'S A WAY ANYONE CAN MAKE COMICS WITHOUT DRAWING A THING! IT'S CALLED...

ALL YOU NEED ARE A FEW BASIC SUPPLIES...

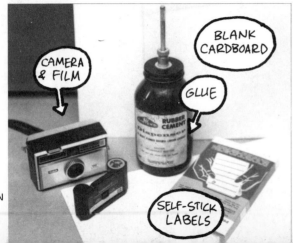

AND SOME ACTORS.

FIRST THINK UP SOME KIND OF STORY TO TELL WITH YOUR COMIC.

THEN WRITE A SCRIPT. THE SCRIPT SHOULD TELL EXACTLY WHAT PICTURES YOU'LL TAKE AND WHERE THE ACTION TAKES PLACE.

A CAREFUL SCRIPT WILL HELP YOU AVOID BAD SHOTS AND SAVE MONEY.

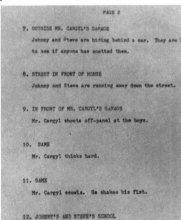

AFTER YOU GATHER YOUR ACTORS, COSTUMES, AND PROPS, YOU'RE READY TO START SHOOTING.

SOMETIMES YOU'LL WANT TO SHOOT DOWN ON THE ACTION...

...AND SOMETIMES YOU'LL WANT TO SHOOT LOOKING UP.

CLOSE-UPS CAN ADD PUNCH.

LAY THE FINISHED PHOTOS OUT IN THE ORDER YOU WANT. YOU MAY WANT TO GET RID OF SOME SHOTS OR TO TAKE A FEW NEW ONES.

FEEL FREE TO CHANGE THE SHAPE OF A SHOT. YOU MAY WANT TO CUT OFF THE UN-NECESSARY PART OF A SHOT.

YOU CAN EVEN MAKE THE IMPOSSIBLE REAL BY CUT-TING OUT PART OF ONE PHOTO AND PASTING IT TO ANOTHER.

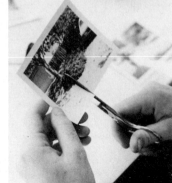

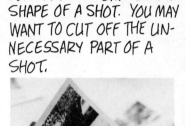

PASTE YOUR PHOTOS ONTO BLANK CARDBOARD PAGES.

THEN WRITE YOUR DIALOGUE ON GUMMED LABELS (OR PLAIN PAPER) AND STICK THEM TO THE PHOTOS. USE SMALL PIECES OF LABEL FOR THE POINTERS.

IF YOUR PICTURES ARE REALLY CLEAR, YOU MIGHT MAKE COPIES OF YOUR BOOK.

NOW COMES THE BEST PART... READING YOUR OWN COMIC BOOK!

How to Put On Your Own "Radio" Plays

It was a big deal when Superman got his own radio show in 1940. In the 1930s and the 1940s before television came onto the scene, radio was the nation's most popular medium. Millions of people listened each day to radio plays featuring detectives, cowboys, spies, reporters, doctors, mounties, lovers, monsters and just about any other kind of character you can imagine.

Imagine was the key word. Radio drama came alive in the listener's imagination. The radio play combined words, music and sound effects to create pictures in the minds of the audience. It was not at all like watching television with the picture off. Radio listeners actually felt that they could see the drama in their minds' eyes.

Today, radio drama just barely survives. Most people prefer to watch and hear the action on television rather than to create their own mental pictures. Except for a few network radio mysteries, the only modern radio plays you're likely to hear are the one-minute dramatized commercials that are popular on many radio stations.

But if you have a tape recorder and some imagination, you can change all this by making your own "radio" plays on tape. Here's how to do it.

Scripting

As with most other kinds of drama, radio plays start with scripts. There are books of ready-made radio play scripts, some taken from the days of old-time radio. But you'll probably have more fun writing your own scripts. You can invent your own plots, or you can adapt short stories, stage plays, even comic books.

Wherever your idea comes from, your finished script will include four things: dialogue, narration, sound effects and music.

Dialogue is what characters say to each other or to themselves. The most important trick in writing radio play dialogue is *tagging*—indicating in dialogue the person spoken *to*:

> EDISON: Do you have the battery hooked up, *John*?
> JOHN: It's connected, *Mr. Edison*.

In this example, John is the tag in the first line. Mr. Edison is the tag in the second line. Tagging is important because the audience cannot see the actors. If the lines were not tagged, the dialogue could be confusing to the listener. Of course, every line does not have to be tagged, but tagging is very important in a scene with three or four characters.

Narration includes the opening and closing speeches of the show's host or announcer. Also, some radio playwriters use a narrator to describe part of the action or to set a scene:

> NARRATOR: Paula finds herself walking between two tall towers, gleaming dull silver in the moonlight. Suddenly, a huge shadow flits across the moon!

Another use for narration is to provide a transition from one scene to another:

> JOE: Let's go!
> SOUND: CAR MOTOR UP, THEN FADE.
> NARRATOR: Ten minutes later, Joe and Phil stop before the courthouse.
> SOUND: CAR HALTS.

A sound-effects man from the Golden Age of Radio does his stuff. Sound effects were responsible for making characters like Superman seem to come alive for the radio audience. Here, the sound man plays recorded effects on the two turntables while preparing to close a door with his right hand and fire a blank pistol with his left.

Narration is a useful tool, but it's usually more interesting to the listeners if as much of the scene as possible is described by sound and dialogue. Stories which are all narration can be very dull, so use the narrator sparingly.

Sound effects—gun shots, phones being dialed, thunder, etc.—add realism to a radio play. Instead of being told that something is happening, the listeners hear it for themselves. Sound effects can also help set the scene. Birds twittering create the image of the countryside. Crashing waves paint a picture of the seashore.

In real life, our eyes often help our ears identify sounds. Noises that are heard but not seen are sometimes hard to recognize. To avoid confusion, radio scripts often have characters comment on the sounds they hear. This is another form of *tagging*:

SOUND: WIND, RAIN AND THUNDER
MARIE: Wow! The rain's really pouring now! How far have we come, George?

The phrase "The rain's really pouring" tags the storm sound effect or "plants it" as some radio writers say.

Music can be used to open or close a program and also to set the mood of a scene. Fast-paced music is good for a chase scene. Romantic music can be played when two lovers are talking. Spooky music can make a mystery play or a science-fiction tale seem scarier.

Music is also used for transitions between scenes. This is called a *bridge*:

COWBOY: Sheriff! Come quick. You're needed in Dodge City.
MUSIC: BRIDGE—UPBEAT TRAVELING MUSIC
RANCHER: Look. Here comes the sheriff.

And sometimes music is used as an exclamation point to end a scene. A crash of music used this way is called a *sting*:

SHERIFF: I'm sayin', Morgan, that if you don't pay your debt by tomorrow noon, you'll end up in jail!
MUSIC: STING

Funny stings, made with slide whistles or silly-sounding musical passages, are called *noodles*. Noodles are used to end comedy scenes.

You can usually find all the background music you need from classical or popular music records. But there are special records available with radio mood music, bridges and stings. You might have more fun gathering your musician friends and making your own music.

The Script

When you type up your radio script, you may want to use some of the techniques that are used by professional script writers. Here are a few of them:

(A) Characters' names are capitalized and set against the margin.

(B) Instructions on how to interpret the dialogue are capitalized in parentheses after the character's name.

(C) Sound and music cues are capitalized and underlined to make it easy for actors, director, sound effects artist and sound engineer (person in charge of the tape recorder) to spot cues.

(D) If a sound occurs in the middle of a speech, the direction is put in parentheses where it happens so that the timing will be right.

Double-space your script. This not only makes it easier to read, but also provides space for writing corrections, actors' notes and the like.

Acting

Because the audience for a radio play cannot see what an actor looks like or does, the actor's voice becomes extremely important.

You can have fun changing your voice to make yourself sound older or younger, confident or nervous, happy or sad, silly or serious, robust or slender. If you have a good ear, you might try to do various accents, if the script calls for it.

Another advantage of acting in a radio play is that you do not have to memorize your lines. The audience will not see you reading from your script. But there is a pitfall here. The dialogue might sound as if you are reading it rather than simply talking with somebody. To avoid this problem, you and your fellow actors should rehearse your lines very carefully until you know the words almost by heart. Then, during the actual performance, you can sometimes look each other in the eye and even make gestures. This kind of interaction, although not seen by the audience, can make your delivery sound more natural and realistic.

Recording

Where and how you record your radio play will largely determine how your final product sounds.

A simple recording studio is easy to arrange. Use a small room that's in a quiet part of your home. The fewer windows, the better, so outside noise will not leak in. If there are drapes, close them. Try putting up sheets or blankets on the walls to deaden the echoes. It helps if the room has a carpet. If it does not, consider laying down throw rugs for the recording session. The cast and crew should take off their shoes to eliminate the clumping and scraping sounds of actors moving toward or away from the microphone.

It is important to use a tape recorder with a good microphone. Put the mike as far from the recorder as possible so it won't pick up the motor noise of the recorder. The mike should be placed on some kind of stand and not held or touched during the recording. Even a slight movement of the mike can put unwanted noise onto your tape. Actors should speak into the mike from about 12 inches to 18 inches away. They should take care not to rustle their scripts.

Sound effects

There are four ways to obtain sound effects for a radio play.

First, you can purchase professionally recorded sound-effects discs at many record shops. By scrounging around, you should be able to find every possible sound from an atom bomb blast to a chicken laying an egg. The difficult part about using sound-effects discs is that they must be cued up on a record player so the sound will be heard at precisely the right moment. Nothing is more awkward in a radio play than a missed sound-effects cue.

The second possibility is to tape record actual sounds yourself. If you have a portable tape recorder, you should be able to capture such noises as traffic, dogs barking, playground sounds and so on. You still have the problem of starting up the prerecorded tape at the right moment.

The third method is to create sound effects "live" during the recording of your play. This requires having someone serve as the sound-effects "artist" who stands ready at a table filled with sound-making devices and materials used to create the noises required by

Adapting a Comic Book Story

You can easily translate comics into radio play scripts. The script to the right has been adapted from the "Shadowfighter" comic strip above.

"Adapted Script"

SOUND: THE ENGINE OF A TRUCK, FAR OFF AT FIRST BUT COMING CLOSER. SOUND CONTINUES AS NARRATOR BEGINS TO SPEAK.

NARRATOR: The muted hum of an engine steals through the silence of a deserted pier...

SOUND: SOUND OF BRAKES AS TRUCK STOPS, ENGINE DIES.

NARRATOR: ...And as a darkened truck rolls to a halt, it is observed by the piercing eyes of a lone figure...Shadowfighter!

SHADOWFIGHTER: (USE AN ECHO EFFECT TO SUGGEST FOLLOWING WORDS ARE SHADOWFIGHTER'S THOUGHTS):

So our mysterious informant wasn't lying. Here they come. And unless I miss my guess, their target will be Denver Ahn!

NUMBER 1: O.K.,boys, surround his quarters. Be ready to attack if I give the word.

NUMBER 3: You want me to go with you, Number 1?

NUMBER 1: No, Number 3, you stay here with the others. Numbers 2 and 4 will go in first with me.

the script. Here are some sounds that are easy to produce:

Fire—Crinkle cellophane 6 inches from the microphone.

Bird flying—Shake a partly opened umbrella up and down.

Breaking down a door—Crunch a piece of balsa wood in a fist held near the mike.

Rain—Trickle grains of rice onto a sheet of paper stretched tightly above the mike.

Telephone voice—Place the mike near the receiver and have the actor talk on the line from another telephone.

Chase through underbrush—Beat two leafy twigs together.

Guillotine—Chop a head of cabbage on a cutting board placed near the mike.

Footsteps on gravel—Have an actor walk in place in a box filled with gravel.

Creaky door—Make a "creak box" from two pieces of wood bolted together. Drill a hole slightly smaller than a piece of dowel. Put a handle on the dowel and insert in the hole. As the dowel is turned, it will bind against the block, making creaks.

Hoofbeats—Clip-clop lightly with styrofoam cups (mouth down) onto gravel or other surfaces. (You'll have to practice to get the rhythm right.)

If you would rather not use prerecorded sounds or work with a sound-effects table, you have one more option. You can create sounds using your own voice.

Strange as it may seem, a real noise may sound less real than the imitation sound you manufacture in your studio. The ear is the final judge. Listen—and keep experimenting!

Coca-Cola

Dr. John Pemberton, inventor of Coca-Cola

Asa Candler, founder of The Coca-Cola Company.

There's an old saying that a *real* salesman is one who can sell water by a river. By that standard, Asa Candler and his followers deserve a spot in the Salesmen's Hall of Fame. By playing on the simple fact that people get thirsty, they turned a bubbly liquid consisting mostly of sugar and water into an empire which circles the globe. That liquid, of course, is Coca-Cola, probably the best-known manufactured product in the entire world.

Strangely, when Coca-Cola started out in 1886, it wasn't intended to quench people's thirst. Dr. John Pemberton, the Atlanta, Georgia, pharmacist who invented the drink, intended it to be a tonic—a kind of all-purpose medicine.

Tonics and homemade medicines were very common in Dr. Pemberton's day. There were no big drugstore chains. Few companies were making medicine. A local pharmacist would mix his own remedies from a lab full of liquids and powders in the back of his store. Pharmacists were always experimenting with new mixtures. Many of these concoctions, called patent medicines, were bottled and sold as cures for everything from headaches to cancer. Because no laws regulated what went into patent medicines, a customer never knew what he was getting. A few tonics may actually have helped people. Most either did nothing at all or were downright dangerous.

Dr. Pemberton wasn't out to poison anyone with his medicines, though he did make some wild claims for them. Two of his big sellers, *Extract of Styllinger* and *Dr. Moffett's Indian Weed*, were supposed to cure a whole list of diseases, including coughs and scrofula. That day in May of 1886 when he mixed up the first batch of syrup for Coca-Cola, Dr. Pemberton was probably looking for a simple "pick-me-up" tonic to be served at soda fountains.

Dr. Pemberton brewed his syrup in a big witch-style cauldron in the back of his shop. He used fruit syrup and extract of South American cola nut, threw in a dash of the leaf of the coca plant and added a handful of other ingredients which became the "secret formula" the company guards to this very day. After heating and stirring the mess, he came up with a nameless, sticky, brown syrup. Dr. Pemberton showed the syrup to the attendant at the soda fountain in Jacobs' Pharmacy. The attendant agreed to test the new drink and mixed the first samples of the still-nameless brew.

The Soda Fountain

Though Coca-Cola has become the world's most famous soft drink, it certainly wasn't the first. Soft drinks (called "soft" because they contained no alcohol) had been around since the 1830s. In 1833 a man named John Matthews invented carbonated water by using pressure to force carbon dioxide bubbles into water. When the pressure was removed, the bubbles were released and fizzed to the surface. Soon after, a French foodmaker discovered how to mix fruit syrups with the carbonated water. The result was soda water, which became an instant hit in America.

By the time Coca-Cola was invented, soda fountains had popped up in cities all over the country. The soda fountains were usually part of the local drugstore. In small towns the soda fountain was often the social center, where people met to talk to friends and drink sodas. Soda fountains dispensed orange sodas, lemon sodas, sarsaparilla, berry-flavored sodas, ginger ale and root beer. Two soft drinks from this era—Hires Root Beer and Dr Pepper—are still around.

In those days, soda fountain owners bought flavored syrups from dealers. The fountain attendant would put some of the syrup into a glass, then fill the glass with carbonated water and serve it to the customer.

Those first drinks may have tasted pretty awful. Legend says that Dr. Pemberton ordered the syrup to be mixed with ice and plain water. The result would have been something like what you get if you let a Coke sit for a day or two until all the bubbles disappear. The fizzy cola we know was invented when an unknown soda jerk (whether accidentally or deliberately nobody knows) mixed the syrup with carbonated water. The new taste was just right.

Dr. Pemberton and his three business partners began selling the syrup to other soda fountains. The four racked their brains for a catchy name for the new product. Finally, bookkeeper Frank Robinson patched coca (leaf) and cola (nut) together to create the famous name. It was Robinson who designed the fancy lettering, or logotype, which still identifies Coca-Cola throughout the world.

Coca-Cola sold, but not very well. Dr. Pemberton still didn't see the geat potential in his new drink. He advertised it as a cure for "insomnia, neuralgia, sick headache, biliousness and indigestion." As a medicine, Coca-Cola was a dud. Pemberton managed to sell a grand total of $25 worth of syrup in his first year in business.

Shortly afterward, the doctor's health began to fail. Whether he tried to cure himself with Coca-Cola is not recorded. Finally, he sold his infant business for $1750. It was up to another man—Asa Candler, the man who mixed Coca-Cola with imagination—to found the company that would make Coca-Cola world famous.

Asa Candler was a wholesale druggist in Atlanta, Georgia, when he bought out John Pemberton's business. Pemberton, now very ill, was happy to unload his drug concern. Candler bought Pemberton's entire line of products, *Extract of Styllinger* and all. But it was the struggling Coca-Cola that really caught his fancy.

Frank Robinson, the logo-designing bookkeeper, joined Candler's outfit. So did Sam Dobbs, one of Candler's nephews. Dobbs suggested the way really to sell Coca-Cola would be to advertise heavily. Candler saw wisdom in the idea and set in motion the first big ad campaign for Coca-Cola. In years to come, not only would Coca-Cola revolutionize the soft drink industry, its promotional campaigns would revolutionize the advertising industry as well.

At first, Asa Candler continued to push Coca-Cola as a medicine, tying it in with his own line of homemade drugs. But an ill wind was blowing for patent medicines. A wave of public pressure was building either to regulate patent medicines or to stamp them out altogether. Had Candler kept pushing Coke as a cure-all, he would have been committing business suicide. The druggist made the smartest decision of his career. He turned Coca-Cola from a tonic for illness into a drink for refreshment.

Business began to boom. Candler and his associates advertised the new drink as no drink had been advertised before. They created banners, change purses, serving trays, calendars and painted signs on buildings. They printed free-drink coupons which entitled someone to walk into a soda fountain and sample Coca-Cola without any risk to the pocketbook. They even came up with the idea of printing the name "Coca-Cola" on the soda fountain glasses in which the drink was served. In 1893 the new advertising campaigns had pushed Coca-Cola syrup sales to nearly fifty thousand gallons. Only seven years had passed since Dr. Pemberton's measly $25 year.

Asa Candler was a smart businessman. He and his associates had turned The Coca-Cola Company into a booming business. But for some reason, he never saw the sense of bottling Coca-Cola.

The first person who realized the possibilities in moving Coca-Cola out of the soda fountain was Joseph Biedenharn, a Mississippi candy-store operator. His customers often asked for a way to take Biedenharn's soft drinks along on picnics and outings. Bottled soda water was already around on a small scale. The storekeeper got into the bottling business by buying a secondhand bottling machine. In 1894 he used the machine to bottle one of his most popular drinks—Coca-Cola. Biedenharn was so pleased with the results that he wrote Asa Candler about his idea and sent him a free case of Coke. Candler wasn't impressed. The king of Coca-Cola sent back a note saying the bottled Coke was "fine." That was all. He didn't even return the empty bottles. Biedenharn shrugged and went on bottling Coca-Cola. Several other independent sellers began to do the same.

Bottled Coca-Cola really came into its own thanks to the foresight of a Tennessee lawyer named Benjamin Thomas. During the Spanish-

The pause that *refreshes*

Drink Coca-Cola

Coca-Cola and Santa

Nothing shows the power of advertising better than the way The Coca-Cola Company's Christmas advertisements changed the image of Santa Claus for millions of people.

Santa Claus, patron saint of children, is based on Nicholas, bishop of Myra, who lived in Asia Minor during the fourth century. Nicholas devoted his life to helping others and became a legend in many countries and cultures. The name "Saint Nicholas" became "Sint Nicoloes" in Germany and "Sinterklaas" in Holland, then finally "Santa Claus."

In 1823, a poet named Clement Moore wrote the now-famous Christmas poem "'Twas the Night Before Christmas." In the poem, Moore called Santa Claus a "jolly old elf." The poem was so widely loved that most artists who drew or painted Santa after that pictured him as elfish and pixie-like.

Then came Coca-Cola. In 1930, The Coca-Cola Company's advertising genius, Archie Lee, decided to use Santa Claus in holiday advertising. He wanted somebody to paint a Santa who would embody all the fun and happiness Christmas held for kids and adults alike. The artist who filled the bill was Haddon Sundblom, a Chicago illustrator. Sundblom painted Santa as a big, warm, friendly, lovable and thoroughly human personality—the sort of person to whom children would love to serve Coca-Cola.

As a model Haddon Sundblom used a retired salesman named Lou Prentice, a man whose face was lined with the happy wrinkles the artist was looking for. Many years later, when Prentice died, Sundblom had aged enough that he used his own face for a model.

The Santa that appeared in the Coca-Cola advertisements became so well-known over the years that eventually almost everybody's concept of Old Saint Nick was based on Sundblom's paintings.

American war Thomas had fought in Cuba. There he saw the popularity of a local soft drink sold in bottles. Thomas remembered his own favorite fountain drink, Coca-Cola, and put two and two together. After the war, he and his friend Joseph Whitehead went to Asa Candler to ask for permission to bottle Coca-Cola nationwide.

Candler could hardly have cared less. He was all for selling syrup to soda fountains, but he still thought the idea of bottling Coca-Cola was a waste of time and money. After Thomas and

Whitehead promised their bottling business wouldn't cost the parent company a cent, Candler drew up an agreement giving the two men the bottling rights for most of the country—for the grand total of one dollar. What's more, even that dollar was never paid!

Gleefully, the two men got a map of the United States and divided the country between them. They knew they couldn't hope to supply the entire nation from their own plants, so they granted local rights to bottlers in each major area. Thomas or Whitehead bought syrup in bulk from Candler's company, then resold it to the local bottlers. The rest, as they say, is history. Bottling Coca-Cola allowed the drink to be sold as never before, and both Thomas and Whitehead eventually became millionaires.

Asa Candler retired from The Coca-Cola Company to go into politics in 1916. A rich man, he sold out his interest in the company. The firm was earning over $13 million a year. Almost the moment the founder left, the company went into a slump.

World War I really hurt Coca-Cola. Sugar was rationed during the war, and when peace returned, sugar prices soared. Since Coca-Cola was nothing without sugar, the company found itself in a price squeeze. To make things worse, the company had to fight one legal battle after another with imitators who were trying to cash in on their drink's reputation. There was Koke Ola, Coca Nola, and the most insistent competitor, the Koke Korporation of America. The Coca-Cola Company spent much time and money before it finally won its case against Koke, taking its argument all the way to the Supreme Court.

Things were looking bad for The Coca-Cola Company. But like the first time the company was in trouble, some people came along with the energy and imagination to turn the company around. One was Robert Woodruff, who became the new president in 1923. Though he was the son of a wealthy man, Woodruff had been forced to make his own

way in the world without relying on the family money. He had worked his way up in the business world with great success. The other half of the new creative team was Archie Lee, a reporter turned ad writer who worked for the agency that handled advertising for Coca-Cola.

Whatever the legendary "secret ingredient" in Coca-Cola may have been at first, for Woodruff and Lee it was advertising. They set out to make Coca-Cola a household word. Their magazine ads, posters, and serving trays showed the drink involved in every kind of day-to-day activity—usually with the picture of an attractive woman to clinch the sale.

When World War II began Coca-Cola was already expanding into foreign countries. The growth stopped when sugar rationing returned. But this time the company was ready. Coin-operated machines were catching on, and a Coke machine went into every defense plant. Determined to take advantage of the war, the company shipped huge quantities of Coke to the fighting forces overseas. Coca-Cola got a real boost in the latter days of the war from General Dwight D. Eisenhower, leader of the Allied forces and a confirmed fan of Coca-Cola. He requested ten complete portable bottling plants be shipped to Europe to supply the advancing Allied armies. The plants followed the armies through German-occupied Europe, were set up a safe distance behind the lines, and thousands of bottles were trucked to thirsty GI's. When the war ended, the company's advanced bottling plants left Coca-Cola in a perfect position to expand throughout the globe. It didn't take long to cover Europe, then to spread into Asia, South America and Africa.

To many people in other countries, Coca-Cola became a symbol of America itself. For better or for worse, the company's operation was so big that this simple soft drink could affect the workings of whole countries.

In the 1920s, the government of Portugal banned the sale of Coca-Cola as a "threat to

In July of 1969, when the first astronauts to visit the moon returned to earth, they were greeted with this giant electric sign.

national health" and a sign of foreign intervention in Portuguese affairs. The ban was finally lifted in 1977. That same year, the Indian government required The Coca-Cola Company to reveal its formula or leave the country. India charged the company with squeezing huge, unfair profits out of the Indian bottlers. They ordered Coca-Cola to turn 60% of its control and all of its know-how over to local firms. The company agreed to part with its control but not with its secrets. When the compromise was unacceptable the company decided to leave India. The Indian government went so far as to hire chemists to develop a substitute beverage. Production of a new "government" drink would give work to the 150,000 Indians who lost their jobs when The Coca-Cola Company decided to close down.

In recent years, Coca-Cola has met stiff competition from Pepsi-Cola, a rival drink which has been around nearly as long as Coke. Pepsi struggled through several periods of near-bankruptcy before finally catching on in the 1940s. In the 1970s, Pepsi actually passed Coke in supermarket sales. Now the two rivals are battling tooth and nail around the globe, even in Russia, where Pepsi won exclusive distribution rights. The Coca-Cola Company is still working to squeeze into the Soviet Union, beginning with a deal that Coke will be the only soft drink sold at the Moscow Olympic Games in 1980.

Coca-Cola has come a long way since John Pemberton. The Atlanta doctor could not have dreamed of the empire that would rise from his backroom tonic. The Coca-Cola Company even has in its files requests from bottlers eager for the first Coke franchise on the moon. It isn't hard to imagine that, before long, the first of those familiar, greenish, contoured empties will appear half-buried in the sands of Mars.

Coca-Cola Through the Years

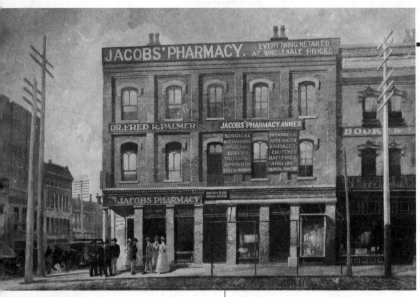

◀ A painting of Jacobs' Pharmacy, where the first Coca-Cola was served.

Coca-Cola and other fountain drinks tried to encourage sales by providing soda fountains with advertising materials to use in their stores. In this picture the fountain has installed mirrors with the Coca-Cola logo and slogans. Glasses, serving trays and glass holders also were made specially for Coca-Cola.
▼

and they MUST go.

Don't think of getting furniture until you go to John Neal & Co. Their prices will suit you.

IVIE,
The Photographer.
PICTURE FRAMES
MADE TO ORDER.

COCA-COLA.

DELICIOUS!
  REFRESHING!
    EXHILARATING!
      INVIGORATING!

The New and Popular Soda Fountain Drink, containing the properties of the wonderful Coca plant and the famous Cola nuts. For sale by Willis Venable and Nunnally & Rawson.

This early newspaper ad for Coca-Cola pushes the drink as "Refreshing" and "Invigorating."

A B C D E F G H I J

The World's Most Famous Package

When Benjamin Thomas and Joseph Whitehead began bottling Coca-Cola in 1899, they had a problem because their soft drink looked like everybody else's. All bottled sodas of the time came in straight-sided glass bottles. Sometimes the name of the drink would appear in raised letters on the side, sometimes not. In a look-alike bottle, Coca-Cola could easily be mistaken for some other soda. Often, when a customer asked for Coca-Cola, the merchant would substitute some cheaper drink, perhaps his own homemade brand. If the customer didn't check the bottle for the brand name, he could easily miss the fact he wasn't getting Coke.

Ben Thomas wanted to find a special bottle for Coca-Cola, one which could never be mistaken. It should be a bottle that could be identified even in the dark, even if the bottle were broken. Unfortunately, manufacturing processes weren't advanced enough at that time to make his wish come true. But a few years later, in 1913, The Coca-Cola Company was ready to look at new bottle designs. One of the interested suppliers was the Root Glass Company, already a maker of Coke's straight-sided bottles. Root's superintendent, a machine designer named Alex Samuelson, thought the new design might be based on the cola nut or the coca leaf. The story is that Samuelson's accountant, T. Clyde Edwards, copied a drawing of the cola nut from an encyclopedia and gave it to Earl Dean, the mold shop supervisor, who then used the nut's shape as the basis for his design. Dean's first bottle was rather fat and would not fit existing machinery. He slimmed it down and submitted the final model to the company. The design was accepted in 1915.

The company had found what it was looking for. There is no mistaking a Coke bottle, even in a crowd of a thousand other soda pop containers. The graceful, practical shape of the bottle won design awards and was even registered as a trademark.

Other soda manufacturers tried to produce their own distinctive bottles. Most were just variations of the straight-sided idea. None ever came close to making the hit the Coca-Cola bottle did.

Pictured above are examples of glass bottles for Coca-Cola, beginning with one of the so-called "Hutchinson" bottles (A) used by Joseph Biedenharn in 1894 in the first Coca-Cola bottling operation. Later (B) bottlers of Coca-Cola began to emboss the Hutchinson bottles with the word Coca-Cola. The Hutchinson bottles used wire hooks to hold the tops on. This made it impossible to drink from the bottle. What's more, the bottles often exploded when they got warm. The transparent and amber straight-sided bottles (C and D) were used from 1900 through 1916, when they were replaced by Earl Dean's new design (E). Since that time the bottle has changed little. Bottle F is from 1923; bottle G from 1937. Twenty years later (H) the molded-in logo was replaced by a painted-on design. In 1961 the first no-return bottle (I) was released. The latest development is the plastic bottle (J), introduced in 1975 and not yet in general circulation.

One of the trucks used to deliver bottled Coca-Cola to stores in the 1920s.

With the growth of bottling came the carry-home carton. The first cartons, introduced in 1923, had closed tops.

A

B

C

D

E

The can for Coca-Cola was born in 1940. (A) The first cans looked like oil cans and had pry-off tops just like the bottles. The cans came in two sizes—16 and 32 ounces— and were just being tested when World War II called a halt to the project.

(B) The Coke can didn't make a reappearance until 1960. The new can contained 12 ounces of Coca-Cola. (C) The can was revised in 1963 and (D) again in 1966. The mid-1960s saw more changes in cans—the pull-tab can was introduced in 1964 and the all-aluminum can came out two years later. (E) A can of Coca-Cola as it appears today.

Dwight D. Eisenhower, a general in World War II and later President of the United States, was a devoted fan of Coca-Cola.

These free-drink coupons were used in the earliest days of Coca-Cola to encourage customers to try the new drink. The coupons were handed out to people on the street who could then trade them in for a drink of Coke at the local soda fountain.

Colored-glass lamps were only one of the many fountain fixtures dreamed up by The Coca-Cola Company. The idea was that no matter what other soft drinks a fountain served, if a customer walked in and was surrounded by advertising for Coca-Cola, he'd be more likely to buy a Coke.

Since its earliest days, The Coca-Cola Company has used advertising to remind people of the product and convince them to buy. The way in which the message was delivered has changed with the times. In 1905 it was "Coca-Cola revives and sustains." In 1911 ads said, "Enjoy a glass of liquid laughter." In 1922, "Thirst knows no season" encouraged people to drink Coke in winter as well as summer. The well-known slogan of the 1970s, "It's the real thing," was first used in 1942.

While the words and illustrations have changed, all advertising for Coca-Cola still fits into a "Coca-Cola style"—cheerful, colorful pictures of people enjoying Coca-Cola.

Advertising Coca-Cola

6,000,000
drinks a day

▲
The bellhop billboard from 1925 pushes the popularity of Coca-Cola by counting drinks per day the same way McDonald's now lists how many hamburgers they've sold.

◀ Coca-Cola became famous for using happy, beautiful people in their ads to suggest the pleasant nature of Coke. This 1923 magazine advertisement reminds people that Coca-Cola can be drunk at Christmas-time as well as on vacation.

◀ During World War II, much advertising for Coca-Cola showed how the drink was becoming known throughout the world. Here an American and a Canadian share a break with Coca-Cola, "the global high-sign." It was during this time that the company finally began promoting Coca-Cola as "Coke." Up until then, executives and ad writers were reluctant to recognize the nickname. But during the war millions of soldiers made the name stick once and for all.

"Welcome, friend"

What Is the Secret Formula?

The "secret formula" of Coca-Cola has caused so much discussion and set so many people to wondering that it's become a full-fledged legend. Some people claim there's no secret formula at all. The Coca-Cola Company claims the formula is kept in a bank vault which can be opened only by a vote of the board of directors. The formula, they say, is known by only three people: the company's two senior chemists and another chemist who has now retired.

One chemist who didn't know the formula decided to try the easy way and analyze the contents of a bottle of Coke to isolate the ingredients which give the drink its special taste. He immediately came up with the information that Coke is 99.8 percent water and sugar. But what about the other 0.2 percent?

Coca-Cola serving trays were used in soda fountains and later at drive-ins. Dozens of different tray pictures were used over the years. Some were paintings like this; others sported photos of popular movie stars. Today the serving trays, like almost all the other promotional products put out by Coca-Cola, have become prized collector's items.

Apparently this is made of caramel (which gives the pop its brown color), caffeine, phosphoric acid, cinnamon, nutmeg, vanilla, glycerin, lavender, lime juice, other citrus oils and extract of a Brazilian seed called guarana. Rounding out the list is the coca and the cola—three parts of coca leaf (minus the cocaine) to one part cola nut. The exact proportion of all these ingredients has not been determined. You will have to experiment with that yourself if you try to make homemade Coca-Cola. Chances are it's less trouble to buy the stuff in a bottle.

Are these really the ingredients, the "secret formula" for Coke? The Coca-Cola Company won't answer one way or the other. They just smile quietly and count up the empties.

Amateur collectors and professional dealers alike hunt for, trade and sell Coke memorabilia. This Los Angeles antique store specializes in nothing but items relating to Coca-Cola. Appropriately enough, it's called "The Real Thing."

The red circle with the famous script is familiar all over the globe, but sometimes the trademark is adapted to the local alphabet. These signs come from America, Thailand, China and Japan.

How to Invent Your Own Drinks

Honey Eggnog

(1 serving)

1 raw egg
½ cup cold milk
2 tablespoons honey
1 teaspoon vanilla
pinch of cinnamon or nutmeg

Blend everything but the cinnamon or nutmeg. Pour the mixture into a glass. Sprinkle the cinnamon or nutmeg on top.

Carrot Delight

(2 servings)

½ cup carrot juice
½ cup milk
¼ cup chopped almonds
2 teaspoons wheat germ

Blend all ingredients.

The Coca-Cola Company hires people whose only job it is to mix up new drinks. One of their recent concoctions is called "Samson," a high-protein beverage made out of cheese whey. ("Whey" is part of what Little Miss Muffett was eating when the spider scared her away. It's the milky liquid residue produced during cheese making.)

But back on the subject of drinks, why let the experts have all the fun? You can create your own beverages by blending some of the dozens of juices available in the supermarket. Lots are ready-squeezed, either in bottles or frozen. Others are stored away in fresh fruits and vegetables, waiting for you to squeeze either by hand or, if you're lucky, by machine.

Don't just plan on combining the good old standbys like orange, apple, grape, grapefruit, lemon, pineapple and tomato juice. How about experimenting with slightly more exotic ingredients, such as the juices of beets, cantaloupes, celery, mangoes, green peppers, pomegranates, papayas and even watermelons?

The recipes given on these pages are meant to inspire you. Some are sweet and fruity; others are vegetable-tasting. Some have special health ingredients (e.g., "high-protein powder") which are good for you but don't add to the flavor.

Most of the drinks were designed to be made using an electric blender. All you do is pour the ingredients in and run the motor

Pineapple-Coconut Islander

(1 serving)

½ cup coconut milk
½ cup unsweetened pineapple juice
1 teaspoon wheat germ
1 tablespoon plain yogurt

Blend all ingredients.

Peanut Splutter

(2 servings)

1 carton (8 ounces) plain yogurt
1 cup milk
3 tablespoons smooth peanut butter
2 teaspoons honey

Blend all ingredients.

Yogurt Creamy

(4 servings)

1 cup plain yogurt
2 tablespoons wheat germ
4 tablespoons shredded coconut
1 banana
2 tablespoons high-protein powder
2 cups unsweetened pineapple juice

Blend all the ingredients.

until everything is blended together. You can probably make most of the drinks without a blender. First you'll have to grind up any lumpy items (like nuts), using either a chopper or a hand grater. Then you'll have to shake all the ingredients like mad. (Make sure the cover is on tight or you'll really get mad.)

Once you get the hang of it, you can start mixing up all kinds of new combinations. When you do, you might consider the following three suggestions from successful beverage inventors:

1) Almost any vegetable juice can be mixed with any other vegetable juice or juices. The combinations are limited only by the juices you have on hand. Of course, many of the mixtures will taste awful. Let your tongue be your guide. Feel free to play around with spices and herbs, such as pepper or oregano.

2) Fruit juices also can be mixed together in endless combinations.

3) If you want to mix vegetable and fruit juices, you probably should use only one fruit juice in the mixture.

When you hit upon a blend that excites your taste buds, the next step is to give it a "grabby" name.

Then, serve your invention to family and friends and challenge them to guess your "secret recipe."

Banana Slippery

(4 servings)

½ ripe banana
1 egg
1 tablespoon non-fat dry milk solids
2 tablespoons honey
½ teaspoon smooth peanut butter
4 cups milk

Blend the egg, milk solids, honey, peanut butter, banana and one cup of milk. Then add remaining milk and blend some more. Can be served hot or cold.

Purple Cow

Contrary to popular belief, there are no purple cows. So, this drink doesn't come from purple cows. Even if there were purple cows, you would probably find it easier to make this drink in the following way:

(4 to 6 servings)

3 cups cold milk from any color cow
1 can (6 ounces) frozen grape juice, partly thawed

Blend milk and grape juice. Pour into ice-filled glasses.

Strawberry Cooler

(8 to 10 servings)

1 pint strawberries
½ cup sugar or honey
2 cups vanilla ice cream
2 quarts ice-cold milk

Blend the strawberries and sugar or honey. Blend in the ice cream and one cup of the milk. Add the rest of the milk.

Garden Guzzle

(2 servings)

½ cup tomato juice
¼ cup celery juice
¼ cup carrot juice
¼ bunch watercress, chopped
1 teaspoon chopped parsley
1 teaspoon lemon juice

Blend all ingredients.

Orange-n-berry Dairy

(4 servings)

1 cup orange juice
1 cup strawberries
1 egg
½ cup dry milk solids
½ cup water

Blend all ingredients.

The Frisbee

The Frisbee, the plastic flying disc that may replace baseball as America's national sport, owes its life to pies and men from Mars.

People have been throwing things since the dawn of time, beginning with rocks thrown at enemies. Somewhere along the way the ball was invented and games like catch followed. Even the throwing of discs goes back quite a ways. The ancient discus of the Greeks is still used today in Olympic competition.

But the flying disc which gave the Frisbee its name was nothing more than a pie tin from the Frisbie Pie Company of Bridgeport, Connecticut. The firm was going strong in the 1920s, when a great many Frisbie pies were eaten by students at nearby Yale University. Whether the pies were any good, nobody seems to know. But the empty tins were great! Students quickly discovered that Frisbie tins, when flipped through the air, would soar like birds. Skilled tin-flippers could even get the pie trays to do tricks, like hovering or returning to the thrower. The new sport was named "Frisbie-ing," in honor of the pie manufacturer.

Years passed. Walter "Fred" Morrison had never heard of Frisbie-ing. Walt Morrison was a California-based carpenter and part-time inventor. Invention ran in the family. Morrison's father had invented the sealed-beam headlight for automobiles. As a boy, Morrison, like most kids, had tried his own hand at pie-tin-tossing, paint-can-lid-hurling and plate-skimming. All this experience might have remained little more

Walt Morrison, inventor of the Frisbee

than a childhood memory had it not been for the flying-saucer craze.

In 1947 Kenneth Arnold, a Washington State businessman, was flying his private plane past Mount Rainier. Suddenly he spotted a formation of nine strange aircraft. They weren't ordinary aircraft. They were discs that flew without wings or engines and disappeared at impossible speed as Arnold drew nearer. When the pilot told reporters about his encounter, he said the mysterious objects looked like "upside down saucers." The newspapers coined the term "flying saucers" and the name stuck. In less than a year, the whole country was flying-saucer crazy. People began seeing flying saucers everywhere, wondering if they came from outer space. The government studied flying saucers. Authors wrote millions of words on the subject.

As the saucer craze grew, Walt Morrison's inventive mind saw a fantastic opportunity. Why not cash in on the mania by making his own flying saucers? Why not turn those tossed pie tins into a full-scale fad? Morrison began experimenting with commercial pie tins in an

Frisbee champion
Margie Meswick

effort to make them more stable. He failed. A metal saucer, Morrison decided, would never work.

Luckily, Morrison lived in the early days of the Plastic Age. Crude plastics had been around for several decades, but it wasn't until World War II that really modern plastics were developed. In those days plastic was looked upon as a miracle substance, the wave of the future. Only after plastic began replacing other materials did people begin thinking of it as "cheap." Walt Morrison took a block of tenite, one of the early plastics, and carved out a cupped disc with sloping, rounded edges—the great-granddaddy of all modern Frisbees. The inventor scrounged up the money to buy a plastic molding machine and went into the flying saucer business.

Morrison sold his first Flyin' Saucers at a Los Angeles county fair. Actually, he didn't sell the discs themselves. He sold pieces of "invisible wire." Morrison and a helper would walk through the fair crowds, holding their hands in the air as if they were carrying a wire between them. "Make way for the invisible wire!" they would shout. Curious fairgoers followed the strange procession. When they reached the booth, Morrison and the assistant pretended to attach the "wire" to two posts. Then the inventor pulled out a Morrison Flyin' Saucer. He had practiced so well that he could send the saucer straight from one post to the other. The disc seemed to be guided by an invisible string. Onlookers crowded around asking how the gadget worked and how they could buy one.

"Oh, I don't sell the saucers," Morrison explained. "I only sell the wire. It comes in hundred-foot lengths for a penny a foot. If you buy the wire, I'll toss in the saucer for free."

The biggest problem with the Morrison Flyin' Saucer was the tendency of its plastic to become brittle when cold. If a saucer hit something hard, like an asphalt street after the sun went down, it would burst into a million pieces. Morrison offered a free replacement Flyin' Saucer to players whose saucers had broken if the owner brought in every single piece. The company had to replace only four saucers.

Despite the shattered saucers, Morrison's toy begain to catch on. He refined his invention in 1951, using a tougher plastic. He still drew heavily on the flying-saucer idea. (This disc had a raised "cabin" with portholes in it.) He named his new model the Pluto Platter. At about that time, Rich Knerr and A.K. Melin were nursing along their small California toy company. Wham-O, as the company was called, specialized in slingshots. In their travels the two men saw many Pluto Platters flying through the California skies. The saucer caught their interest, and they tracked down Walt Morrison. History was made when Morrison, Knerr and Melin signed on the dotted line. Wham-O bought the Pluto Platter design and began to produce the first of over one hundred million flying discs that have filled the heavens during the last twenty years.

The Pluto Platter's popularity grew slowly. The saucer was pushed aside in 1958 when Wham-O's miracle product, the Hula Hoop, caught on. The new fad nearly killed the Platter. But the Wham-O people were sure they had a hit on their hands. They went on sales trips throughout the country. One of them took Rich Knerr close to Yale University, where he heard of the legendary Frisbie tins and the sport of Frisbie-ing. Knerr liked the name and decided to use it for the Wham-O saucer. However, as he had only heard but had never seen the name, he misspelled it "Frisbee." The new name was first used in 1959.

In the early 1960s, Ed Headrick, the vice-president of Wham-O, came up with the refinement that saved the Frisbee's life. He found that by putting raised "flight rings" on the saucers, the Frisbee would be more stable and accurate. Headrick pushed the plastic disc as a sport, not just a toy, and his strategy worked. The Frisbee shot to fame in the middle and late 1960s and has been going strong ever since.

Headrick himself went on to start the International Frisbee Association, as well as one of the first Frisbee "Guts" teams. Before long, there were more Frisbee teams, then more games, then tournaments, then world championships. The IFA now has a grading system by which a Frisbee thrower can work his or her way up from "Novice" to "World Class Frisbee Master."

A team of professional Frisbee performers has traveled with the famous Harlem Globetrotters basketball team, entertaining crowds with astounding Frisbee feats. There are championship contests for Frisbee-catching dogs, and several areas have set up Frisbee golf (Folf) courses.

Of course, in the decades since the first Wham-O Pluto Platter was introduced, many other companies have come out with their own plastic flying discs, including the Zolar, the Gyrospin Gee-Whizzer, the Psychedelic Comet, the Hasbro-Glo, the Belly Button and the Tosserino. Frisbee addicts have tested all of them with a complicated set of standards measuring throwing ease, accuracy, stability, hovering ability and how well the discs resist turning over in flight. A chart published in 1974 listed forty-eight separate models, topped by Wham-O's "Super Pro" model. The Frisbie pie tin which started it all placed forty-first.

While fans and game-players were looking to Frisbees for fun, the United States Navy injected a more sinister note. The story leaked out that the Navy Department was trying to adapt Frisbees to carry flares for combat and rescue use. At the time, flares were attached to parachutes. But the chutes drop straight down and land quickly. A Frisbee might cruise over a target, offering light for much longer.

Project N00164–49–0662 was born in 1969 at a cost of $375,000. According to news stories, the Navy tested Frisbees in wind tunnels. They tossed endless Frisbees and followed the flights with computers and special cameras. Finally, researchers figured that if a Frisbee flare were launched at just the right speed, it would supply a respectable 20 seconds of light. The project was moved to Utah. The Navy built a complicated Frisbee-launching machine on the top of a cliff and fired the first flare-saucers into the air. Unfortunately they had made a miscalculation. Once the flare was lit, the burning material acted like a rocket engine. Instead of soaring gracefully over the ground, the flaming Frisbee shot straight up into the air.

When the story leaked out, many people were disturbed. Most Frisbees were sold to people between the ages of 18 and 30, who, at the time, wanted nothing to do with the military. Wham-O was afraid that drafting the Frisbee into the military would kill its sales forever. They needn't have worried.

After the project was canceled, the Navy revealed that the "Frisbees" in the experiment weren't Frisbees at all. In fact, no plastic flying discs were ever used in the Navy project. Instead, the flares were specially made saucers of a claylike substance. An inventive report writer thought the word "Frisbee" was more convenient than saying "flat flying flare saucer" over and over.

Frisbees fill the air above Washington, D.C.

A close catch in a Guts game

All kinds of people play with Frisbees

Something to shoot for

Members of the International Frisbee Association break distance records every year. The men's throw record is over 410 feet. The women's record is just over 280 feet. The maximum-time-aloft record is just short of ten seconds. For a real challenge, try the run-throw-catch. Toss the Frisbee, run along with it and catch it when it comes down. The men's distance record is over 230 feet; the women's 140.

FRISBEES

How to Throw a Frisbee

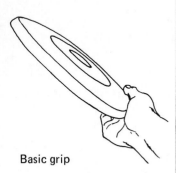

Basic grip

Frisbee tossers use dozens of different throws and catches. These range from the simplest techniques to elaborate trick shots only an expert can do. Here are the basics of throwing a Frisbee. Once you have them down pat, you can work on fancier throws.

The basic Frisbee grip. Hold the Frisbee comfortably in the palm of your throwing hand. Your first finger should rest along the rim of the Frisbee. The other three fingers curl underneath. Your thumb is on top of the Frisbee.

Backhand toss

The *backhand toss* is one of the most common Frisbee throws. Turn your shoulder toward the target. Extend your arm so that your index finger points where you want the Frisbee to go. Bring your throwing arm back, bending your elbow and cocking wrist around. Then straighten your arm. At the moment your arm is fully extended, let the Frisbee go with a snap of the wrist. At the same time take a step forward with your right foot (if you're right-handed). At the end of the throw your finger should be pointing at the target.

The key to accurate throws is to keep the Frisbee as flat as possible when you let it go. The flatter your throw, the straighter the Frisbee's path will be. When you start out, throw at a target that isn't too far away; 25 or 30 feet will do. Once

Underhand toss

you've perfected your short-range aim, begin moving the target back.

Another popular throw is the *underhand toss*. Face the target squarely, your arm pointing where you want the Frisbee to go. Use the same basic grip. But this time bring your arm behind you until it's nearly parallel to the ground. To toss the Frisbee, bring your arm forward, bending the elbow slightly as your hand comes under. Extend your arm, launching the Frisbee with a flip of the wrist. As you throw, take a step forward with the foot opposite your throwing arm (the left foot if you are right-handed). Once again, try to keep the Frisbee on a level, flat flight path.

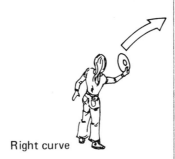

Right curve

Left curve

Even if you are a beginning Frisbee thrower, you have probably learned how to throw *curves*. You simply tip the disc as it is released. To make the Frisbee's flight path curve to the right, toss the disc with the left side up and the right down. For a left-hand curve, keep the left side of the Frisbee lower than the right.

How to Catch a Frisbee

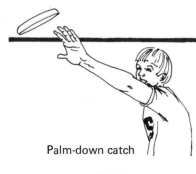

Palm-down catch

Palm-up catch

A proper Frisbee catch is a one-handed catch. Trapping the Frisbee between both hands may be O.K. for rookies, but you will never win many points that way.

There are two basic Frisbee *catches*: the palm-down and the palm-up. In either case, the idea is to let the Frisbee sail into the little pocket between your thumb and forefinger. When the Frisbee hits, close your hand around it. Usually, the palm-down catch is easiest when the Frisbee is above your waist; palm-up catches are better when the Frisbee is coming in low. However many players make it a point to catch everything with the palm down, simply because it *is* harder.

Inventing fancy catches is one of the Frisbee fanatics favorite pastimes. There are hundreds, including the behind-the-back catch, the between-the-legs catch and the one-finger catch, in which the Frisbee is snagged on the tip of the index finger. When you have mastered the basic catch, start trying harder ones. Stancil Johnson's book, *Frisbee*, shows many other catches and throws.

Behind-the-back catch

Master
Proficiency Rating Qualification

THROWING REQUIREMENTS

NOTE: Examiner please initial each group as completed.

GROUP 1   Four Straight Flights   X_____

GROUP 2   Four Right Curve Flights   X_____

GROUP 3   Four Left Curve Flights   X_____

GROUP 4   Four Hover (or Floater) Flights   X_____

GROUP 5   Four Skip Flights   X_____

GROUP 6   Distance (40-yd. min.) Throw 1 _____ yds. up-wind
           (four consecutive)   Throw 2 _____ yds. up-wind   Average _____ yds.
                                    Throw 3 _____ yds. down-wind
                                    Throw 4 _____ yds. down-wind   X_____

GROUP 7   Self-caught flights (two consecutive)
           1) MTA (6 sec. min.)   OR   2) Throw, Run & Catch (80 ft. min.)
              Throw 1 _____ sec.   Throw 1 _____ ft.
              Throw 2 _____ sec.   Throw 2 _____ ft. X_____

GROUP 8   Overhand Wrist Flip Deliveries Four _____ Flights
                                           Four _____ Flights   X_____

GROUP 9   Alternate Style   Four _____ Flights
                                           Four _____ Flights   X_____

CATCHING REQUIREMENTS

Four consecutive catches with right hand   X_____
Four consecutive catches with left hand   X_____
Three consecutive behind-the-back catches   X_____
Three consecutive between-the-legs catches   X_____
Three consecutive behind-the-head catches   X_____
Three consecutive finger catches   X_____
Three consecutive tip catches   X_____

FRISBEE MASTER CERTIFICATION

NAME:_____ IFA#_____

has qualified in all the requirements for the rank of FRISBEE® Master
as attested by:

IFA Member_____ IFA#_____

IFA Member_____ IFA#_____

IFA Member_____ IFA#_____

MASTERS CERTIFICATION FEE $7.50

THIS_____ DAY OF_____

61

How to Train Your Dog to Catch Frisbees

A man's best friend is his dog, and a dog's best friend is his Frisbee. Or so you may think once your own dog is an accomplished Frisbee-snagger. The performances of Frisbee catchers like Hyper Hank and Ashley Whippet have thrilled fans throughout the world. While you may never win any prizes, you can still have a lot of fun teaching your dog to catch flying saucers.

The first thing to do is get your dog accustomed to a Frisbee. Let him play with it. Use the Frisbee as a food or water dish.

Once your dog is used to plastic flying saucers, use a Frisbee (preferably an old battered Frisbee) for a game of tug-of-war. Dogs love to tug on things. A Frisbee tug-of-war will get your dog accustomed to having the Frisbee in his mouth.

Now slowly roll the disc past your dog. When he runs after the Frisbee, give him encouragement. This and all the steps in dog-training should be done only when your dog is eager and fresh. If the dog loses interest or gets tired, give up for a while and try again later.

Now you're ready to teach your dog to leap for the Frisbee. Hold the disc just out of reach so your dog has to jump for it. Before long, he will be making higher and higher leaps.

The next step in the training routine is to play *keep-away*. Play catch with a friend, sailing the Frisbee slow and low over your dog's head. He'll chase the Frisbee and perhaps even jump and catch it. Remember, don't tire your dog out or try to continue after he loses interest.

Hyper Hank at the Rose Bowl

Ashley Whippet bites off just what he can chew

Now you're ready for a game of *fetch*. Hold the Frisbee just out of reach, as you did for leaping practice. But when your dog starts to jump for it, take several quick steps backward and throw him the Frisbee. Chances are he will catch it. Encourage him to bring the disc to you; then continue the game. Before long your dog will be chasing long throws and nabbing them in the air.

You may be surprised. Who knows? Your mutt's shaggy hide may conceal the abilities of another Ashley Whippet (seen at right), one of the superstars of the Frisbee dog world.

FRISBEES

How to Play Folf

The Eleanor Pardee Park Folf Course

Folf, or Frisbee golf, is a great test of accuracy and distance throwing. Plan your course like a regular golf course. Set up nine or eighteen holes. Instead of cups and flags, use buildings, trees and the like for targets. You can make things even more challenging by introducing obstacles which require you to throw your Frisbee through tunnels, between tree limbs or maybe over low buildings. For experienced players an average hole is between sixty and a hundred yards from "tee" to target. At first, less skilled players will want shorter distances between holes. Vary the length and the difficulty of the holes. Some should be long and open, calling for good distance tossing. Others should be short enough so that a good, accurate throw could score a hole in one.

Have several people play the course a few times. Then figure out the average number of throws needed to complete each hole. This is the "par" for the hole. Most holes should have a par of three or four tosses.

Here is a sample course designed around a small park in Palo Alto, California. Your own Folf course could be in a park, a school yard, a farm—anywhere.

Eleanor Pardee Park is a small park on the corner of Channing and Center Streets in Palo Alto. The park is surrounded by trees. (The trees along the edge have been left out of the drawing right for clarity's sake.) In the middle is a large clearing. Our Folf course is of easy-to-medium difficulty and has a lot of trick shots. A close look at it will give you some ideas when you lay out your own course.

1st HOLE. 48 yards, par 3. Tee off from the big wooden "Eleanor Pardee Park" sign toward the fenced-in tots' play area. First player to tee off is the one who can tell the best story about who Eleanor Pardee was. If nobody knows, flip a coin. Land the Frisbee in the cage on top of the tots' slide.

2d HOLE. 25 yards, par 2. Tee off from the sidewalk opposite the four cement crawl pipes. Toss the Frisbee through the pipes and land it in the spring-mounted rocker near the fence.

3d HOLE. 40 yards, par 3. Tee off from the rocker. Hit the sign that says "All dogs must be on leash, P.A.M.C. 6.16.100." If the Frisbee lands on a dog not on a leash, score an automatic hole in one.

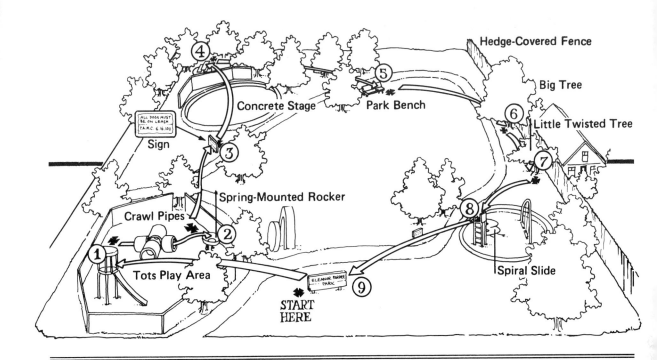

4th HOLE. 55 yards, par 3. Tee off from the other side of the sign toward the wood backstop behind the concrete stage. Your target is a picnic table on the other side of the backstop. You have to squeak the Frisbee between the top of the backstop and a low limb. Since you can't see the table from the tee, it's a good idea to have someone make sure nobody's eating there before teeing off.

5th HOLE. 77 yards, par 4. Tee off from the table. Land the Frisbee on the park bench beyond the cluster of trees. It's a straight, easy throw for an accurate tosser, but if you throw only curves, your Frisbee will be bouncing off a lot of trees.

6th HOLE. 76 yards, par 3. A nice distance shot. Tee off from the bench and hit the big tree next to the hedge-covered park fence. Be careful not to send your Frisbee over the fence. The neighbors' dogs may not be friendly, and they are not on leashes, either.

7th HOLE. 16 yards, par 2. This hole is for players who have been frustrated by the last six holes. Tee off from the big tree and hit the little twisted tree 48 feet away. Relax and toss an easy hole in one.

8th HOLE. 37 yards, par 3. Tee off from the small twisted tree toward the slide and swing area. Land the Frisbee on top of the platform on the spiral slide. Getting to the slide isn't hard, but the platform is surrounded by a can-like guardrail. It is tricky to land on unless your first shot lands at the foot of the slide; then you can cheat by just flipping the Frisbee into the can.

9th HOLE. 62 yards, par 3. Tee off from the platform on the slide. Your target is the park sign from which you started. Watch out for the trees, and you will have no trouble. Now add up your score and see how close you come to the par of 26. You did the course in half that? In that case, it's time to come up with a tougher course.

How to Play Guts Frisbee

Guts Frisbee

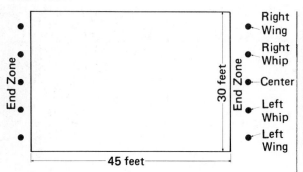

A flying catch in a furious Guts game

Guts Frisbee is played on a field 15 yards long and 10 yards wide. There are two teams, usually of five members each, although the game can be played just as well with more or fewer players. For each player added or subtracted, add or take off 6 feet from the width of the playing field. Each team lines up in the end zone behind their goal line. One Frisbee is used.

The object is to score points by throwing the Frisbee past the opponents' goal line without its being caught. All throws must be within the 10-yard width of the field. No throw may be higher than the farthest reach of the players. All catches must be one-handed. Any number of players may touch the Frisbee as long as it is in the air, but once the Frisbee hits the ground it is dead. Catching a Frisbee after it bounces off the ground is not permitted. More than one person may catch the Frisbee at the same time, so long as each player has only one hand on the Frisbee. The last receiving player to touch the Frisbee must be the one to return it. However, if a shot goes out of bounds, the team chooses which player will throw.

An uncaught Frisbee in the receivers' goal space gives the throwers one point. A throw above the upstretched arms of the receivers gives the receivers one point. The receivers also get a point if the toss goes outside the side boundaries. There is no back boundary to the end zone; the Frisbee may be caught anywhere behind the line. Game is 21 points. In the event of a 20-20 tie, the winner must win by two points.

The throwing team in a Guts match must play on the receivers' weakest points. Weak catchers will find most of the Frisbees coming right at them. Fast shots and fakes also help. But remember, out-of-reach throws give the other side a point. Keep the Frisbee within reach (6 to 8 feet, depending on the players' ages).

Receiving teams should use teamwork to make difficult catches. Very seldom does the first player to touch the Frisbee make the catch. Often a receiver will bat the Frisbee down, block it or bounce it so that a teammate can make an easier catch. Grandstanding by trying to make a tough catch alone is likely to give the other team a point. On high shots, receivers must reach for the Frisbee, but they need not jump for it if it is out of reach.

A referee decides disputed points. If there is no referee, both teams are expected to be honest and call their own faults.

How to Stage a Frisbee Relay Race

This race is a variation on the old relay foot race. The Relay is run by two teams. An open field is all right for a playing area, but it's usually more fun to run the race around something like a school building so that only a few players can see the Frisbee at any one time. Each team spreads out in a circle around the building. The team in the inside circle will have a slight advantage because their circle will be shorter. You can even things up by keeping the two circles as close together as possible or by having the inside team make their starting throw slightly after the outside team.

At the beginning of the race, the starting player of each team has a Frisbee. When the referee signals, each starter throws to the next player in the circle. The object is to be the first team to pass the Frisbee all the way around the circle back to the starting player.

If a pass is not completed, the Frisbee must be retrieved by the nearest player and tossed to the last thrower to restart the relay. A player may back up or go as far outside the circle as necessary to catch a pass. He must then return to his position before throwing to the next player. If a player sees a toss is going to fall short, he may not advance toward the thrower to catch the disc. The would-be receiver must let the Frisbee land, then return it for another try. It is illegal to interfere with the throws or catches of the other team. It is also forbidden to deliberately block someone trying to recover a stray Frisbee.

It's a good idea to use a different colored Frisbee for each team. Otherwise, in the excitement of the race, a player may accidentally catch the wrong disc. If at the end of play it is discovered the teams have exchanged Frisbees, the race doesn't count and must be done over.

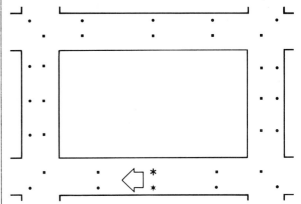

Frisbee Relay

The Frisbee Relay Race requires teamwork and fast, accurate throws. The longer a toss takes to reach the receiver and the more time spent chasing missed Frisbees, the longer it will take the disc to go around the circle. Make quick, sure catches, and then pass the Frisbee immediately to the next player in as straight a line as possible.

Television

Philo T. Farnsworth at age 13.

The person riding the horse-drawn hay mower across the Idaho farmland was Philo T. Farnsworth. He was thirteen years old, and as he went up one row and down the next, an incredible idea was taking shape in his brain. It had to do with electronic circuits, magnetic fields and vacuum tubes. The more he thought about it, the more he knew it was possible. He knew how to build the world's first practical television system.

Television! The word was still so new in the 1920s that most people had never even heard it. Science fiction writers of the time were still writing about the magic of radio, an invention that was hardly out of the testing stage. Television was almost beyond dreaming about.

But not for Philo. Though only a high school freshman, he was already a professional inventor. A year earlier he had won a national inventor's contest by developing a burglar-proof car lock. The prize was $25.00, a lot of money for the Farnsworth family. More important than the money, though, was the proof that Philo could invent things that other people would find useful.

Philo's early life sounds like a story written for the movies. He was born in 1906 in a log cabin in Indian Creek, Utah. His parents were poor Mormon farmers. When Philo was six, his father brought home a gramophone, an early kind of non-electric record player that ran by winding up a spring.

After Philo heard about Thomas Edison and Alexander Graham Bell, he decided then and there that he wanted to become an inventor. He would not waver from that goal for the rest of his life.

Magicians do not really pull rabbits out of empty hats. And inventors do not pull inventions out of empty heads. They almost always build on the earlier efforts of other inventors. And so it was with Philo T. Farnsworth.

When Philo's family moved from his birthplace in Utah to the Idaho farm—taking all their possessions in three covered wagons—eleven-year-old Philo discovered a pile of old science magazines in the attic. He read about the problems inventors around the world were trying to solve. And it was there, in the pages of those discarded *Science and Invention* magazines, that he first read about television.

For over thirty years, scientists had known it was possible to send a picture electronically from one place to another. Electrons could carry the picture along in a kind of code, the way electrons carried a voice message in the telephone wire.

The problem someone had to solve to make television a reality was breaking up the original picture into little pieces that could be sent along the wire one at a time. Put more simply, the trick was to build a camera that could "read" a picture bit by bit rather than all at once the way a photographic camera does.

In the 1880s, the French artist Alfred Robida not only predicted the invention of television, but also suggested some of the ways it would be used, including education (top) and personal communication (below).

The device being experimented with before Philo became interested in television was a spinning metal disc punched with holes designed to break up the picture. A European named Paul Nipkow had invented this kind of mechanical blinking system that worked, but not very well. As Philo read about it, he realized that the proper solution would be an "electrical eye" that would move back and forth across a scene the way the human eye reads lines of print in a book. The invention Philo imagined would have no moving parts. The camera would read—or scan—the scene under the control of electromagnets.

During the next few months, Philo worked by himself, figuring out details of the device he would someday call "the image dissector." It wasn't really that he wanted to work all alone. There just wasn't anyone he knew who could help him with the problems he was puzzling over.

Then late one winter day, he decided to share his ideas with his high school chemistry teacher, Justin Tolman. Philo sketched his invention on the blackboard while the teacher watched in amazement. Tolman told Philo that he thought the device would work, but that it would take a great deal of money to make it happen. Most of the parts would have to be created from scratch since Philo's drawings called for equipment that had not yet been invented.

Still, Philo was glad that he had confided in his teacher. It was important at the time to have discovered someone who could understand. Almost fifteen years later he learned how really important those few hours were when it came time to prove who actually was the inventor of electronic television.

Philo knew that all the giant electronic companies were racing against each other trying to be the first to develop television.

Farnsworth, at age 21, with his "Image Dissector" tube and transmitter. This picture was taken September 1, 1928, two days before the *San Francisco Chronicle* announced Farnsworth's invention to the world.

(They weren't racing against Philo. They didn't even know he existed.) But without money, there was nothing the young inventor could do. He knew he had much to learn and spent every spare minute in study, to be ready when his chance came. He worked as a railroad electrician and took correspondence courses from the University of Utah. At age fifteen, when his family moved back to Utah, he attended college—now calling himself "Phil" because he thought it sounded more mature. When his father died the next year, he left college and went to work. He continued his education with mail order courses while contributing to the family income with a variety of odd jobs, such as repairing and selling radios. This was electronics in a way, but a far cry from television.

Then the big break came. A fund-raiser from California was hired to organize the local community chest drive. The man, George Everson, recognized Phil as a hard worker and hired him to help out. Phil recognized George Everson as the kind of person who knew how to get money when he wanted it. By the time the job was over, Phil had convinced Everson and his partner to raise money for the development of television. It would only cost $5000, promised Farnsworth.

A few months later, Everson had lined up some bankers and other investors to support Phil's work. A lab was found above a garage on Green Street in San Francisco. There Phil, his new wife Pem and his brother-in-law Cliff Gardner set to work. The money people gave them a deadline of one year.

Invention, said Thomas Edison, is one percent inspiration and ninety-nine percent perspiration. The Farnsworth team was now about to find out how true that was. Often they worked through the day and then through the night. There were few ready-made electronic parts available. When they needed a special kind of tube or circuit, they usually had to make it themselves.

Always they were afraid of spies who might steal their ideas, so they worked as secretly as possible. To the people in the neighborhood, the bunch of inventors looked downright suspicious. Once, in the earliest days of their research, one suspicious neighbor called the cops, and there was a raid on the laboratory. The police could not make much sense out of all the tubes and wires. It all looked mysterious. But, fortunately, having a mysterious-looking lab was not against the law.

Then, just before noon on September 7, 1927, the team was ready to try out the equipment. Cliff Gardner was in one room with the transmitter. In front of the camera he put a glass slide that had a single black line drawn on it. When Phil called from the other room that his receiver was on, Cliff opened up the camera lens.

Vladimir Zworykin, promoted by RCA as the "father of television."

The four members of the Green Street crew who produced the first all-electronic television picture on September 7, 1927. Top right: Carl J. Christensen with the camera; center: Philo T. Farnsworth; bottom left: Cliff Gardner with the receiver; bottom right: Robert Humphries.

Farnsworth, with the rest of the staff, watched the fist-sized round, flickering blue screen. Suddenly a dark line appeared. "We've got it," yelled Phil. "Now tip the slide a bit."

Slowly the picture on the screen shifted. "When that happened," said Mrs. Farnsworth years later, "we knew that we were definitely seeing the line in the other room."

For about fifteen minutes, everybody jumped up and down. Farnsworth rushed out and sent a telegram to the investors in Los Angeles: "The damn thing works." Then everybody went back to work, trying to improve the picture.

A few months later, the investors all gathered in the lab for a demonstration. Phil pointed to the blank screen and said, "This is something a banker will understand." When he turned on the equipment, the picture of a dollar sign appeared.

In the months ahead, it was harder to keep their work secret. Newspapers began publishing stories about the breakthrough. One day, a famous East Coast scientist named Vladimir Zworykin came to visit the lab. Seven years earlier, Zworykin had tried to develop his own version of all-electric television. But the equipment hadn't worked, and the government refused to grant Zworykin a patent. The scientist, in fact, had gone back to experimenting with the spinning-wheel approach to television. Now, as Phil courteously showed him around the lab, Zworykin realized that he had gone off the track. An all-electric approach

Philo Farnsworth recording results of experiments in his laboratory journal. Like most professional inventors, Farnsworth kept a detailed running account of the developments and ideas that occurred during the course of his work. Also each of his co-workers kept a notebook.

to television was possible. Here it was in operation. Zworykin, pointing to the equipment, told Farnsworth, "I wish I had invented that." Then he left. A few weeks later he went to work as the head of RCA's television research force. Phil wondered out loud if he had shown Zworykin too many secrets. He would soon find out.

The work continued, but more slowly than the Farnsworth team had expected. Some of the financial backers were impatient to get their money. The project had already cost more than $25,000. The bankers wanted to sell the invention fast to a big company. But Phil wanted more time to perfect it himself. The investors were even more upset when the Great Depression came, making it unlikely that the mass of people would have money to purchase television sets even if they were available.

In 1931 Farnsworth moved most of his team to Philadelphia, Pennsylvania. There he joined the Philco Company. Later, working independently, his team put on a public demonstration of television that amazed people from near and far. The team also began a series of experimental broadcasts over the air.

And then, just as it seemed that success was within grasp, RCA sued Farnsworth claiming that he had stolen his ideas from Vladimir Zworykin. Suddenly, Farnsworth's energy was taken away from inventing and directed to answering the charges made by his giant competitor.

For years the matter was fought in the courts, but finally, Farnsworth won the last of the battles. Perhaps the deciding bit of evidence in the battle came when Phil's old high school teacher, Justin Tolman, testified that he had seen Phil's diagrams almost twenty years earlier, long before Zworykin and RCA even claimed to have been working on television.

But despite Phil's victory, he was not widely recognized as the inventor of television. His contributions were largely forgotten as other inventors and companies helped to perfect the device. In the late 1940s, RCA became the leading manufacturer of television sets, though to do so, they had to pay for the use of over a hundred of Farnsworth's patents. Yet, whenever RCA told the story of the invention of television, they talked about Vladimir Zworykin, not about Farnsworth.

Phil, however, was not concerned about fame. He wanted to focus his efforts on his current projects, including ways to harness fusion power—the power of the sun. When people asked him how he felt about not receiving attention, he used to say, "I can't be bothered. Let the historians take care of that." And they did. On the fiftieth anniversary of the day all-electric television first worked, news programs around the country finally carried the true story. Millions of people learned about Philo T. Farnsworth . . . on TV.

Week Ending Oct. 19, '29 It was found this week the the present dissector work best on not less than 500 volts. We have been using only 135 V. This was inadvertently, of course. Using the new amplifier and the improved oscillight of figure 29, a picture can be transmitted which is much better than any which we have previously been able to handle. A photograph of "Pem" from the receiving end is included for reference in plate figure 30.

IMAGE TRANSMITTED
OCTOBER 21, 1929.
EXPOSURE APPROX. 15 SEC.

FIGURE 30.

Lubcke continued his work on the characteristics of the oscillight. He has suggested that the element be modified somewhat over that shown in figure 29. He suggests putting the filament shield right over the top with only a small hole, and making the grid merely a small ring.

A sample page from Farnsworth's journal dated "Week Ending Oct. 19, '29"—ten days before the Great Depression would begin. This entry discusses a breakthrough in picture quality. Figure 30 (middle of the journal page) shows the image quality obtained two years after the original transmission of a straight line. This is a photo of a televised picture of Farnsworth's wife and co-worker, Pem. The second paragraph, opposite the picture, describes the work of Harry Lubcke, one of Farnsworth's associates.

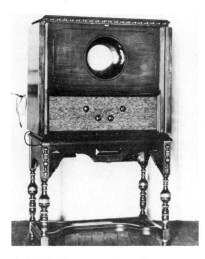

A 1930s Farnsworth receiver was packaged in a wood cabinet suitable for marketing. But the Great Depression and World War II would keep sets off the market until the late 1940s.

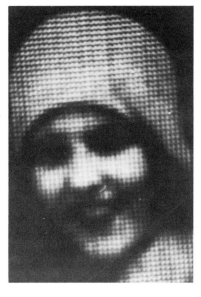

It took six years to improve the picture quality to acceptable standards. The blurry face of the woman (left) was televised in 1930. The relatively clear shot of the child (above) was photographed off the screen during a 1936 experiment.

How Television Works

You may have played the game of making pictures by filling in squares on a piece of graph paper.

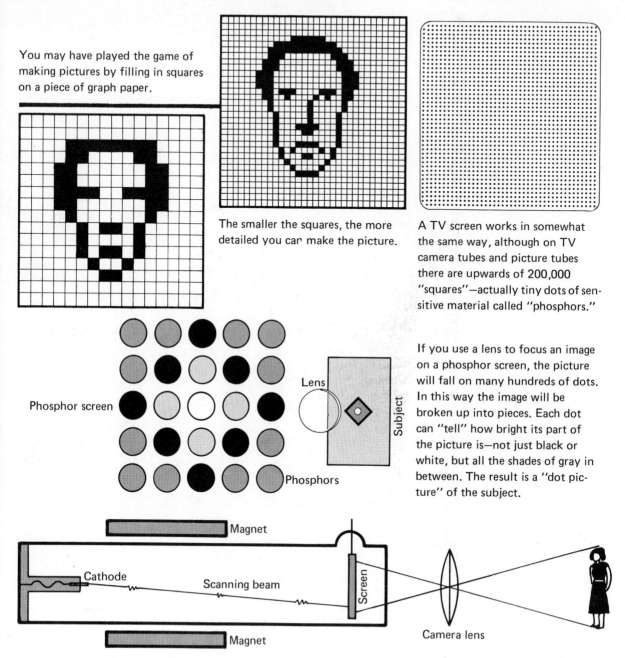

The smaller the squares, the more detailed you can make the picture.

A TV screen works in somewhat the same way, although on TV camera tubes and picture tubes there are upwards of 200,000 "squares"—actually tiny dots of sensitive material called "phosphors."

Phosphor screen

Lens

Subject

Phosphors

If you use a lens to focus an image on a phosphor screen, the picture will fall on many hundreds of dots. In this way the image will be broken up into pieces. Each dot can "tell" how bright its part of the picture is—not just black or white, but all the shades of gray in between. The result is a "dot picture" of the subject.

Magnet

Cathode

Scanning beam

Screen

Camera lens

Magnet

In a TV camera, the picture is focused on a sensitive phosphor target. A tiny electronic "gun" called the *cathode* shoots a *scanning beam* at the target. Magnets make the beam scan back and forth like a searchlight, moving over the phosphors, row by row, faster than any eye could follow. As the beam moves, it reads how bright each phosphor is and translates that information into a stream of electrical impulses.

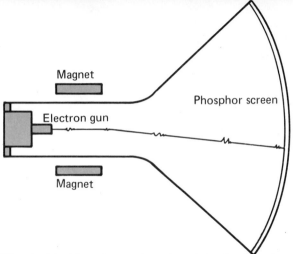

Magnet

Phosphor screen

Electron gun

Magnet

The electrical impulses are broadcast into the air and are picked up by your home TV set. Inside the TV tube is another electron gun, scanning the screen at the same speed as the camera beam. The electrical impulses tell the beam how brightly to light each phosphor on the screen, one by one.

The screenful of glowing dots re-creates the picture in black and white. Because the beam scans the whole screen 30 times every second, your eye can't see it move. The brain sees a constant picture. And because the dots are so small and so close together (there are 525 rows of dots on a TV screen) the eye can't see them either.

If you play with colored lights, you will find that blue, green and red lights overlap to make white. Blue, green and red are called "primary colors." This means that any color there is may be created by some combination of these three.

How Color Television Works

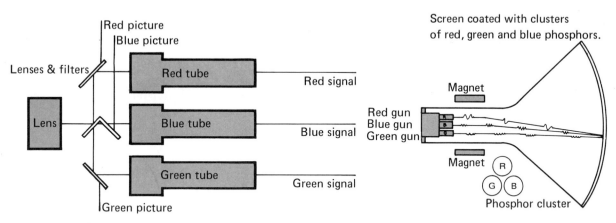

Red picture

Blue picture

Lenses & filters

Red tube — Red signal

Lens

Blue tube — Blue signal

Green tube — Green signal

Green picture

Screen coated with clusters of red, green and blue phosphors.

Magnet

Red gun
Blue gun
Green gun

Magnet

R
G B

Phosphor cluster

The color TV camera uses this principle to make colored pictures. Using filters and mirrors, the camera makes three pictures of the subject. One picture shows how much blue is in the colors of the subject; one shows how much red, and one shows how much green. The three pictures are all sent through the air just like a black and white picture.

In most color TV tubes, there are three electron guns instead of one and clusters of three phosphors—red, green, and blue—on the screen. The red signal "tells" the red gun how bright to make each red dot on the screen; the green and blue work in the same way. Again, the phosphors are so close together and so small that instead of seeing patches of red, green and blue dots, the eye sees the whole range of colors.

Feast or Famine?

Action on the local news

News consists of dramatic events, behind-the-scenes accounts (documentaries) of happenings, interviews with important people, and commentaries which explain what the news means.

Within a few years after the start of commercial television broadcasting in 1947, most of the kinds of shows we know today were already on the air. The titles and actors might change from season to season but there was always drama, news, sports, comedy and so on.

Nearly all the formats were borrowed from radio. During the 1930s and 1940s, radio presented quiz programs, children's hours, mysteries, comedies and song shows, as well as news and sports. Even the famous TV show *Candid Camera* was inspired by a radio program called *Candid Microphone*.

Nowadays some people look at television and call it a wasteland. Others marvel at the variety of programs available. "There's something for everybody," bragged a top television executive. Perhaps what is seen depends on the eye of the beholder. Check out the following program gallery. What do *you* see?

P.S. Many of the categories overlap. For example, a children's show can be educational; so can a newscast or a quiz show. In fact, people have learned life-saving techniques while watching medical dramas.

Drama has been part of television from the beginning. In the early days, many individual plays were broadcast. Now the emphasis is more on dramatic series with continuing characters. Either way, the drama has taken many forms.

Historical drama—*Poldark*, part of the PBS *Masterpiece Theatre* series

Interview of Nobel Prize winner Alexander Solzhenitsyn by CBS News Correspondent Walter Cronkite.

Police action *Kojak*

Melodrama—*Family* series

Situation comedy seeks out what is funny in realistic or far-fetched situations. Over the years, comedies have spoofed the police, family life, school, spies, cowboys, the good old days, the army, the rich and the poor.

The Honeymooners

Laverne & Shirley

Game and quiz shows are popular with broadcasters because they are easy and inexpensive to produce. Most of the prizes are provided free by companies who want publicity. Shows that use people from the audience cost even less. Even if the contestant wins several thousand dollars, that's less than what a Hollywood star charges for an appearance.

Producers never seem to run out of ideas for game shows. They've had contestants try to name songs, guess people's jobs, do stunts while racing the clock, guess the price of products and try to solve picture puzzles. The heyday for quiz shows occurred in the late 1950s with programs like *The $64,000 Question*. The bubble burst when some quiz champions admitted that they had been given the answers before the show.

In *Family Feud*, two families compete by answering questions on a wide variety of topics.

Concentration requires a good memory and picture-puzzle solving skills. The best contestant, from the producer's point of view, is one who shows a lot of enthusiasm. Sometimes contestants are coached backstage on how to grimace, shout, groan and scream.

Sports was the subject of the first commercial television program—a Dodgers-Pirates baseball game broadcast from Ebbets Field in Brooklyn, July 1, 1941. Year in and year out, sports have remained one of the most popular kinds of programming. Television's ability to get in close and to replay action on videotape has created much more knowledgeable fans. Some people believe the excitement generated by televised contests has encouraged young and old people to get more involved in sports as active participants.

The emotional side of a basketball game becomes evident when the camera shows the facial expressions of the players.

Television puts the viewer in the middle of the action of even the fastest, most dangerous sports like auto racing .

Children's programming has received more attention in recent years than most other areas of broadcasting. Many people claim the shows are either dull or overly violent. Some blame parents for using the tube as a babysitter. Others are convinced that any television viewing for any reason is harmful because it teaches children to be passive spectators. Those who study history, however, point out that the same criticisms have been made of earlier entertainment media, including radio, movies, comics and even (believe it or not) books.

Variety shows, as the name suggests, can include all kinds of acts, but usually feature singers, dancers, comedians and musicians.

The Tom and Jerry/Grape Ape Show features animated cartoons.

Live animals and animal puppets help little kids learn about the world on *Captain Kangaroo*. The "Captain," Bob Keeshan, appeared as the clown Clarabell on TV's first popular children's show, *Howdy Doody*.

Hamming it up on the *Donny & Marie* show.

The Captain & Tennille Show on location in New Orleans.

Baking "Tartes aux Fruits" with Julia Child on *The French Chef*.

Educational television has instructed viewers in everything from car repair to algebra to tennis. Thousands of students have earned college credits by participating in televised courses. Others were satisfied simply to learn how to fix a leaky faucet.

Getting an earful on *Sesame Street*.

Fine arts include classical music, ballet, opera, painting, sculpture and architecture. Television has given people in small towns or people unable to afford expensive tickets a chance to see the best performers in the world.

Opera star Beverly Sills as "Anna Glawari" in all-new English language version of *The Merry Widow*.

Mikhail Baryshnikov and Gelsey Kirkland in ballet performance at Wolf Trap, near Washington, D.C.

Religion has been part of television programming since the earliest days. While most religious programs appear on Sundays and holidays, there have been prime-time religious shows. The most famous was Bishop Fulton J. Sheen's *Life Is Worth Living*. Sheen's program in the early 1950s competed successfully with the antics of Milton Berle, who was television's first superstar.

Father Miles Riley hosts *I Believe*, a San Francisco program where guests step out of their professional roles to share their own personal goals and convictions.

The Rating Game or: How Come They Cut Your Favorite Show?

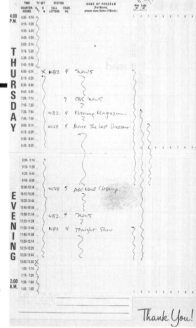

Why do some shows stay on the air for ten years or more while others go off—are *cancelled*—after only a few weeks? The answer is simple: numbers.

Most shows are paid for by sponsors. The sponsors want to reach as many people as possible with their messages. They don't want to pay for shows that are not popular.

But how do sponsors figure out how many people are watching their programs? The first step is easy. They hire specialists to do the counting for them. These research experts, of course, cannot ask all the people in a town or across the country what they are watching. Instead, the researchers select at random a small number of people—called the *sample population*—to represent all the viewers in a given area. Studying the sample population gives clues about the real population in much the same way that studying a model airplane can tell you what the full-size airplane looks like.

The important thing is to make sure that the sample population really reflects the actual population. For example, if one-third of the viewers are people over fifty-five years old, the sample should have about one third of its members over fifty-five years old. If twelve percent of the actual population is black, the same percentage of the sample should be black.

Mathematicians know that the sample size is the key to making the sample population match the real population. Imagine, for example, that you have a box of 1000 marbles. Half of them is green. One quarter is red. The other quarter is blue. If, with your eyes closed, you pick only four marbles, there's

The Audilog diary determines who is watching which programs. It separates out each household member's viewing so that the researchers can tell which programs appeal to children or adults or both.

a fairly good chance that you will come up with three or four green ones. That sample would not accurately reflect the actual mix of marbles. But if you draw out 100 marbles for your sample, you are almost guaranteed to get about half green, about one quarter red and one quarter blue—just like the full-size population. The larger your sample, the better the odds are that it will closely resemble the full-size population.

So the researchers want to make their samples big enough to be accurate. At the same time, they do not want them to be too big because bigger samples cost more money and take more time to count.

One of the most famous audience-counting companies, A. C. Nielsen, uses a sample of 1200 households to represent the 68 million households in the United States. The Nielsen experts believe they can accurately describe

The Storage Instantaneous Audimeter electronically charts household television use. At least twice daily a computer "talks" to the 1200 Audimeters placed around the country and uses that information to reveal what programs millions of Americans are tuned to.

what shows are tuned in on millions of sets by studying only what is happening in 1200 homes. (Nielsen does not always use the same households. Each year some new ones are added and others dropped. But the number is always about 1200.)

To find out what the sample households are tuned to, the Nielsen Company pays a small fee for the right to attach an electronic device to each television set in the house. The device, called a Storage Instantaneous Audimeter, is connected to a computer in Dunedin, Florida. Twice a day, the computer "phones up" each Audimeter in each of the 1200 households and finds out what programs have been tuned in. If, for example, half of the sets have been tuned to a given program, then the Nielsen Company reports that half of the television sets across the country were tuned to that program.

The Audimeter does not, however, tell *who* is watching or even if anyone is watching. It merely reports channel settings. To find out exactly who is watching what, the Nielsen Company places diaries in the homes of another sample group. People in these homes receive a small payment for writing down the names of the programs they watched during the course of a week.

What counts, in the end, are numbers. How many people or sets were tuned to a given program determines the future of that program. No one measures how strongly the viewers feel about the program. For example, one show may have ten million viewers, most of whom think the show is just O.K. Another program may have five million viewers who really love to watch it. But in a head-to-head competition, the first show will win the rating game.

Only rarely will a relatively unpopular show be kept on the air. The most famous example is *Star Trek*. When its ratings fell below the cutoff point, the network announced plans to drop the program. Within a few weeks, thousands and thousands of viewers sent their protests to the network and to the sponsors. The fans generated so much noise and publicity, the show was brought back for another year.

Moral: When your favorite program is about to be cut, SCREAM!!!!!!!

. . . And Now a Word about Sponsors

JOE KOLL for KRONOS WATCHES

Nearly one-fourth of all commercial broadcast time is filled with advertisements. Early commercials cost as little as $9.00 a minute. Now a minute of time may cost as much as $100,000!

Commercials very rarely tell out-and-out lies. But they do use a number of tricks to make viewers remember their products and to shape the way people feel about their products. One way to avoid being fooled by advertising techniques is to keep on the look-out for such tricks. If you recognize them, they probably won't fool you. Here's a list of techniques to watch out for. As an experiment, you might see how many of them you can spot during a single evening of television viewing.

Testimonial

A sponsor may hire a celebrity to speak on behalf of a product. Famous movie stars or national figures sometimes get a million dollars or more to appear in a few commercials. When a famous person claims to use the product himself or herself, it is called a testimonial. What many viewers fail to consider is that the celebrity may know even less about the product than the ordinary citizen and is seldom an expert concerning the sponsor's product.

Flattery

One of the oldest ways to manipulate people is to flatter them—tell them how smart, how good looking or how terrific they are. It's exactly how the swindlers in *The Emperor's New Clothes* sold the emperor an "invisible" suit of clothes.

Omission

Advertisers often tell you how their product will solve a given problem—for instance, settle an upset stomach or clean up the linoleum. But they almost never tell you about other ways to do the same job. These other solutions might be cheaper or better or both. (For instance, eating fruit and exercising to overcome constipation.)

Association

The sponsor may try to connect the product with something the viewer already feels good about, even though the product really has nothing to do with that other thing. Over the years, products have been linked to everything from rocketships to favorite songs to the U.S. flag.

Audience Involvement

Did you ever notice that if someone leaves a sentence half finished, you have a strong desire to complete the phrase? Most people do not like to see things left hanging. Advertisers may use this fact by leaving part of their pitch unspoken, hoping that the viewer will complete the phrase in his or her own mind, where it really counts.

A related technique is to ask a question that the viewer will want to answer. For example, following the demonstration of a safety feature in a car, the announcer may ask, "Isn't this the kind of safety you want for your family?"

Irritation

Strange as it seems, we sometimes remember things that upset or annoy us more than we remember pleasant things. This is why some commercials feature nasty, stupid, screechy or otherwise irritating characters or demonstrations. You may hate the commercial but end up remembering the product the next time you are in the store. One toilet paper commercial, that almost everyone hated, was the most successful toilet paper commercial of all time. (It was rumored that even the sponsor hated the commercial but agreed to run it when tests showed that it convinced people to buy the product.)

Context

To make a product seem better or more desirable than it really is, the advertiser may show it in a setting different from real life. For instance, a commercial may picture someone eating a bowl of cereal in a beautiful garden, next to a babbling brook. Or beautiful music may be played in the background after someone with a headache has just swallowed a headache tablet.

Slippery Words

Advertising writers are masters at using vague or misleading words and phrases that seem

to promise something but really do not. For instance, "none better" does not mean that the product is the best. It just means that no other product is better. "Improved" does not mean that something is good. It could still be lousy but just not as lousy as it was before. And "new" doesn't mean "terrific." Air pollution is relatively new but most people don't think it's very good.

Humor

When people are laughing, they feel good and their defenses are down. So advertisers often use humor in their commercials. Often it's the sponsor who has the last laugh.

Scary Talk

Fear is a powerful mover of people. Advertisers often try to make viewers afraid of something—smelling bad, not being up to date—so they can then offer them a product or service to solve the problem.

Repetition

Other things being equal, studies show that the more often something is repeated the more likely it is to be remembered. No wonder advertisers try to repeat the name of a product as often as they can without seeming repetitious. One way to disguise repetitions is to create dialogues in which characters discuss the product, the product, the . . .

Miracle or Monster?

Mary Shelley's great horror classic *Frankenstein* begins with Dr. Frankenstein conducting electrical experiments that he hopes will benefit the world. As everyone knows, instead of creating a miracle Frankenstein invents a monster.

Many people today believe that television, originally presented as a marvel, in reality is an evil force. Almost daily, writers find new ways to attack the tube, charging it with everything from promoting crime to misrepresenting the elderly.

One book referred to television as "the plug-in drug." Another demanded the total elimination of the tube, arguing that even educational programs cause more harm than good. (Some families got rid of their sets and wrote articles declaring that they are happier and healthier than they were when television was in their lives.)

Science fiction writers have churned out numerous anti-TV stories. In one, the television news people go about causing great calamities just so the evening news will be interesting. In another, contestants on a game show are hunted down and killed on camera—the ultimate in sports action.

The film based on Mary Shelley's *Frankenstein* is a favorite on late-night television. This poster was made some time after the movie starring Boris Karloff opened in 1931. We know it was "after" because Karloff's name was withheld until the opening (to which he was not even invited).

Television on Trial

Despite the many obvious benefits of television (many elderly people have called it their "only friend"), large numbers of parents, teachers, police officers, doctors, lawyers and ordinary citizens have formally condemned television. Here is a list of their charges.

Whether or not television is really guilty of all these crimes remains to be seen. The "trial" is likely to last a long time. Evidence is still coming in on both sides. But you don't have to wait for the official verdict from psychologists, educators, doctors and other scientists. Judge for yourself. Study the charges. Think about how television operates in your life, in your family's life and in the lives of your friends. Make up your own mind whether the "electronic Pandora's box" is a miracle that should be praised or a monster that should be banished.

Television wastes time

The average American spends about four hours in front of the television each day. Over a lifetime, that adds up to be nearly nine years. That time could be spent learning new skills, traveling, reading, doing things with friends and family, living life to the fullest.

Television sells people things they don't need

The average television viewer sees more than one hundred commercials a day. Because the ad people know how to be super-persuasive, they are able to sell viewers things they don't really need. Millions of people are disappointed that the products do not make them happy the way the commercials promised they would. Untold others suffer a worse fate—they fall deeply into debt.

Television has caused a decline in reading scores

Children do not read as well as they used to mainly because they do not read as much as they used to. Instead of reading, they watch the tube.

Television misrepresents reality

Most programs show that social problems are so uncomplicated that they can be solved within an hour. They show that the bad guys cannot be reasoned with. They often suggest that using violence is the best—maybe the only—way to solve problems.

Television teaches passivity

Instead of playing sports, singing, dancing, going out and doing things, many television viewers sit or lie around watching other people live active lives. Viewers forget that there is a difference between firsthand and secondhand experience.

Television is a health hazard

People who spend a lot of time in front of the television do not get enough exercise. That adds to their risk of heart disease. They also tend to watch television in positions that harm their posture. They get fat partly because eating is the only "activity" that is easy to do while watching programs. Meanwhile, excessive viewing causes eye strain and fails to give the eyes sufficient exercise. In addition, the artificial light and rays emitted from the set may be harmful. Also, viewers often fail to get enough natural sunlight and fresh air. Finally, according to a poll of doctors, television can cause nightmares.

Television weakens the imagination

With reading, you have to use your imagination to "see" characters, scenes and actions. But television pictures leave nothing to the imagination.

Television interferes with family life

Instead of talking together, eating together, playing together, working on projects together, many television-addicted families focus their energies on the screen, not on each other. They know their television heroes better than they do their own family members.

Television inspires violent acts

In several cases, people have committed unusual crimes similar to ones shown on television. Some criminals have even testified in court that they got the idea for their crimes from television shows.

Television makes people indifferent to actual violence

People see so much pretend violence on television, they get used to it and almost accept it. There have been stories of groups of people standing aside watching someone being attacked without doing anything to help—watching as if the real violence were a television show.

Beyond the Channels

While people argue over the kind of television programs that enter our homes, there are whole other worlds of television currently in use or being developed. United States businesses alone are producing about 50,000 programs a year for their own use in training workers, communicating to customers and so on. That is more TV than the four major networks produce. Television is becoming an increasingly important tool in education, science and technology. Whether *these* uses are good or bad remains, literally, to be seen.

Security

Television cameras act as additional "eyes" in protecting homes and businesses from intruders. Such systems not only help police catch suspects but also may discourage potential criminals.

Education

Videotaped programs can be used in classrooms at just the moment the teacher and the students are ready. Videotape even makes it possible for television programs to be played for a single student.

Videodating

A woman watches the videotape of a man she may decide to go out with. She is taking part in the newest way for people to meet other people: videodating.

Video Art

For some artists, the television screen is a new kind of canvas that can be "painted on" with electrons. The artists usually work with computers to make startingly complex and ever-changing designs and patterns, as in this "video weaving" by Berkeley, California, engineer Steve Beck. Using his invention called a "direct video synthesizer," Beck can "paint" with over 4000 colors.

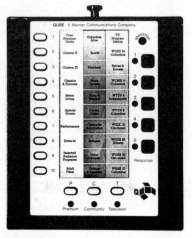

Medicine

Television has been blamed for causing a wide variety of ailments, everything from bad posture to broken bones (kids trying to imitate superheroes leaping from upperstory windows). So perhaps it is fitting that doctors are trying to harness the tube for research, diagnostic training and even treatment.

In the photo shown here, Stanford University eye doctors are experimenting with a television eye test that can be used for mass screenings for eye disease. People taking the test at home will write down their responses to visual sequences appearing on the television set. Certain answers indicate eye problems that even the viewers may be unaware of. Early identification can save many people from blindness, and in some cases, even from death.

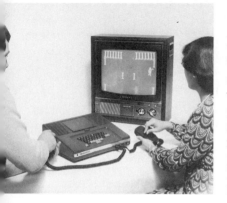

Play

The marriage of computers and television produced the video game. Here, the computer creates pictures and movements that challenge the reactions of viewers who can play games ranging from basketball to gladiatorial combat.

Voting

A new cable television system called QUBE allows subscribers to talk back to their TV sets by pushing "response buttons" on a hand-held control box. Viewers can answer quiz questions, bid in auctions, vote on issues of the day and second-guess coaches during sports events. The system even allows viewers to decide the fate of programs.

One night the announcer on a rock show asked the audience if he should finish the show. People all over town pushed response buttons. The computer counted the votes. Then the emcee said, "The majority says we quit. The majority rules. Thank you and good night." The show went off the air.

Information Display

Television screens are now used as "electronic blackboards" to display information in airports, hospitals and even in the home. Here, the screen displays data about the user's family budget as figured by a small home computer. Shortly, according to the experts, people at home will be able to read anything they want—from the day's news to best sellers to ancient manuscripts—simply by punching in the right code.

Two-way Communication

It is now possible for individuals or groups in different cities to meet face to face using a video telephone. This system allows people not only to talk to each other, but also to show each other art work, photographs, charts, graphs and other objects. Just as important, it makes it possible for people in distant places to "read" the faces and the gestures of the people at the other end of the line. Sometimes a grin or a wink or a scratch of the head can communicate as much as words.

The picturephone service is used mainly by businesspeople, but individuals, too, can use the system. It costs about $6.00 per minute from San Francisco to New York (not all cities are connected yet). But for those who haven't seen loved ones in a while, the charge is worth it.

Distant Visions

From the Greek *tele* meaning "distant" and from the Latin *vision* meaning "sight" we get our word *television*—"distant sight."

The people who have taken the word television most literally are the scientists at the National Aeronautics and Space Administration (NASA), who have used television to see millions of miles across space. Their pictures go beyond news and beyond entertainment. They give people on earth a new understanding of the universe and our planet's place in it.

NASA's use of television as a tool for communication, research and exploration comes close to Philo Farnsworth's vision of what the medium could—and should—become.

Scientist-Astronaut Joseph Allen, an Apollo 15 spacecraft communicator, is holding a photograph of the lunar surface while viewing the actual "moon walk" of Astronauts David Scott and James Irwin on his television monitor.

Astronauts Neil Armstrong and Edwin Aldrin, Jr. (on right with hand saluting flag) shortly after their arrival on the moon. The lunar module is in the background; a metallic U.S. flag "waves" in the foreground, between the two astronauts.

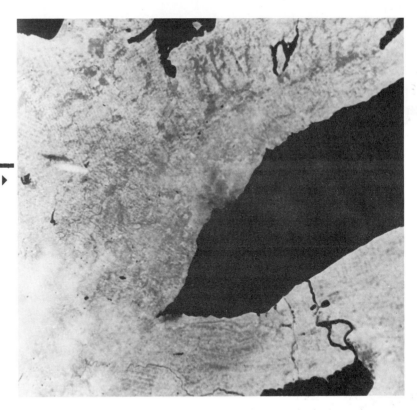

The Toronto, Canada-Buffalo, ▶
New York area as seen from 914
kilometers (568 miles). This com-
posite photograph was transmitted
via television from the Earth
Resources Technology Satellite-1
(ERT-1). The satellite uses highly
accurate cameras called "remote
sensors" to study vegetation on
Earth. Data collected is studied
by experts in agriculture, forestry,
geology, land use management,
hydrology, meteorology and
pollution.

Some of the notable geographi-
cal landmarks shown here are:
Lake Ontario (center right); Lake
Erie (bottom right); Toronto,
Canada (center); Buffalo, N.Y.
(lower right); Hamilton, Canada
(at extreme left on Lake Ontario);
Niagara River (lower right be-
tween Lake Ontario and Lake
Erie); Niagara Falls (midway
between lakes on Niagara River);
Welland Canal (to left of Niagara).

Overall view of the crowded
Mission Operations Control Room
following recovery of the Apollo
13 crew. A large TV screen in the
background shows the ceremonies
aboard the prime recovery ship, the
USS Iwo Jima, thousands of miles
away in the Pacific Ocean.
▼

The sun has cool spots—at least ▶
relatively speaking. The different
shadings, in this electronically
coded picture beamed to Earth
from an orbiting solar observatory,
indicate regions of varying heat
intensity. The hottest areas appear
white.

How to Put Yourself On

In the years ahead, television cameras and videotape equipment will be more common in homes and in public places, such as libraries and schools. You will probably have many chances to make your own TV programs. That can prove to be a lot more fun than watching television programs made by professionals.

Amateur set-ups usually have only one camera, so you won't be able to do the complicated things you see on commercial television. But there still will be plenty of room for creativity. Here are a few suggestions for the kind of programs that can be done well with a single camera and a videotape recorder.

Variety show

Television is great for showing off a variety of stage skills because it brings the audience up close. Viewers can see the juggler's nimble fingers, marvel at the magician's dexterity, and closely inspect the ventriloquist's lips.

Your main job will be locating the talent. That shouldn't be too hard since almost everybody can ham it up one way or another, whether it's telling a bunch of corny jokes,

High school students in Mechanicsburg, Pennsylvania, are producing a series of videocassette programs describing their school's vocational education program. The tapes will be played for junior high school students in the area.

Audio-visual librarian Jay Peyser tests out the portable video equipment available on loan to residents of Huntington, New York.

skipping through tongue twisters, making a rabbit disappear, playing a saxophone or doing a mind-reading act.

Every variety show should include at least one singer. Happily, he or she does not have to have a great voice. A non-singer can delight an audience simply by miming a song—moving the lips as if singing while, off camera, a record or tape provides the actual music. This was a popular kind of act in the early days of television and is still used in commercials when the advertiser finds an actor with a pretty face but an ugly voice.

Preparing a song-mime routine is quite simple. First, you select the record you want to mime. Next, you rehearse it until you have the pacing and the breathing down pat. Then you rehearse the gestures you want to make during the mime. Perhaps you will want to pace around a bit, pick up a vase of flowers during the song, make a gesture. Some songs suggest a costume—for instance, "Singing in the Rain" or "I've Been Working on the Railroad."

During the production, you will want to play the recording close to the microphone so it will sound the way it would if you were actually doing the singing. The effect will be quite convincing unless you're a female miming a song by Frank Sinatra or a male trying to get away with a rendition by Barbra Streisand.

Sports

With a single camera it is hard to capture football, soccer, basketball and other sports that use large playing areas. But if you want to make your own sportscast, there are plenty of other small-scale sports and contests that will make excellent subjects. Some possibilities that will allow you to come close to the action are: marbles, table tennis, hopscotch, darts, blindman's bluff, jacks, running bases and maybe even steal-the-bacon. Whatever sport you choose, be sure to accompany your video portion with a lively, informative and at least occasionally humorous narration.

Children's Program

If you want a really appreciative audience, try making a show for young children. They will be less critical than adults, mainly because they have seen less. Lots of things are still new to them.

Children's shows have been around since the beginning days of commercial television. Usually they include such bits as: puppet plays, songs, skits, stories (the camera may show the pictures of a book while someone reads the words), riddles, jokes, demonstrations of how things work (a faucet, the TV) and demonstrations of how to do things (make a paper airplane, draw a picture).

The best children's shows give the viewers something to do while the show is actually on. For instance, you might demonstrate how to do "backsies" with a jump rope and then invite your audience to try it along with you. You can ask viewers to sing along (there once was an adult show called *Sing Along with*

Mitch), to guess the answers to riddles, to play "Simon Says," to make sound effects that go with a story you're reading, to sew something, to repair something.

Most successful kids' programs feature a character who runs the show: a captain (Captain Kangaroo), a scientist (Mr. Wizard), a teacher (Miss Frances), a neighbor (Mr. Rogers) or a magical guide (Mr. I—Imagination). These characters often wear distinctive costumes. Making costumes for your show can be a great part of the fun. Note, also, that characters can also take the form of puppets (Howdy Doody) or pretend animals (Big Bird).

Teleplay

Human beings might be called "the story-telling" species. Throughout history, people have used spoken words, gestures, drawings, photographs, sounds and movies to tell stories. Television is merely the most recent of the means for sharing tales.

The difficult thing about producing one-camera television plays is that you cannot easily cut from one actor to another or from one scene to another, things which are easy to do in multi-camera studios.

The trick, therefore, is to plan your play pretty much the way you would plan a stage play. Try to arrange for the action to flow in large chunks. Don't crowd too many people into one scene. For best results, keep the script simple.

Of course, you can use the camera's zoom lens to come in for a close-up when you want to show an actor's facial expression or when you want to show the detail of a prop—perhaps a piece of treasure or a secret message.

Naturally, if you are videotaping your production, you can stop the tape and move to another location. By taping in various places, especially going from indoors to outdoors and then back again, you can add great visual interest to your play.

As with nearly all other kinds of plays, the television play script is important. This kind of script has two parts. The first, called the "video," describes what the camera will show. It includes directions for the actors and also tells how the camera should be moved. *Zoom in* means to come close by adjusting the lens. *Zoom out* means to move away from the actors by adjusting the lens in the opposite direction. If the camera is on a wheeled platform, called a dolly, it can be physically moved in closer or rolled back away. *Pan* means to swing the camera right or left, the way a person turns his or her head to one side or the other. *Tilt* means to point the camera up or down. A *close-up* is a televised picture in which one person's face fills up the screen. A *long shot* usually shows the overall setting. A *medium shot* usually shows people from the waist up.

The "audio" portion of the television script describes the words spoken by the actors or the narrator. It can also tell what sounds should be heard (thunder, traffic) and what music should be played.

To see how this all fits together, study the portion of the sample script (on next page). For your own shows, you will probably want to write your own scripts based on stories or plays you have read, incidents that have happened to you or ideas that just popped into your own head without even being invited in.

Video	Audio
1. Woodsy background. Long shot.	1. From off screen we hear whistling of Little Red Ridinghood.
2. Same as #1. Little Red enters from right. She is carrying a basket of goodies.	2. LITTLE RED: (whistles)
3. Same as #1. Wolf enters from left.	3. WOLF: Hello there, little girl. LITTLE RED: A talking wolf?
4. Same as #1. Camera zooms in to medium shot (head and shoulders)	4. WOLF: What did you expect? A parrot? LITTLE RED: Boy, are you nasty.
5. Same as #4. Wolf makes an aside.	5. WOLF: You ain't seen nothing yet. LITTLE RED: What was that?
6. Same as #5.	6. WOLF: I said, Where are you going with all those goodies?
7. Little Red makes a face at him. She says her line then sticks her tongue out at him, then exists left.	7. LITTLE RED: That's for me to know and you to find out.
8. Zoom in closer on wolf. We see the book in the wolf's hands (paws). It's a picturebook of LITTLE RED RIDINGHOOD. Wolf then heads off to right. Camera stops on sign that reads: This way to the short cut.	8. WOLF: I think I already know. Ha! Ha!

- end of scene -

Video Mirror

A videotape set-up is like a mirror with a memory. You can use it to see and hear yourself the way other people see and hear you. A videotape can show you what you look like when you're walking, riding a bike, jumping rope, sleeping, trying to hit a baseball, diving, talking, just sitting there smiling, laughing, thinking, giving a speech or doing anything else you like or hate to do.

Viewing yourself this way can help you get to know yourself better and can even help you improve certain skills. Some people find this use of videotape very entertaining. Others find it upsetting. But almost no one finds it boring.

Behind the Scenes of the Six O'Clock News

First thing in the morning, the *news director* (behind the desk) calls a meeting to discuss which stories should be covered during the day. Some are follow-ups to stories done earlier. Other ideas come from articles in the morning newspaper or leads uncovered by reporters on their beats. For example, there is usually a reporter at city hall ready to keep up with political news. Finally, some stories begin with tips phoned in by ordinary citizens.

Teletype machines print out stories on what is happening in other parts of the country and around the world. The station pays a fee to news gathering services like the Associated Press (AP) and United Press International (UPI) so they can use these stories on the local news program.

The *assignment editor* matches reporters and camera crews with stories that need to be covered. Like fire fighters, crews at the broadcasting station wait, ready to head out to the scene of a fast-breaking story. Using radio or telephone the assignment editor can contact reporters in the field and direct them to newsworthy events. The chart in the background (right) helps the editor keep track of his crews.

Cartoons, charts and other illustrations often play a part in the presentation of news stories. The station's *graphic artist* will create pictures suggested by the reporters. Sometimes, of course, a picture used in one story can be used weeks or months later if a similar story comes along.

As the hours go by, activity picks up in the main newsroom where reporters and editors write up their stories.

Do you ever watch the credits roll by at the end of a show? Why does it take dozens and dozens of people to put on a program where only a few people appear on the screen?

While every kind of show is different, all television shows require teamwork. To see for yourself, join us behind the scenes of the six o'clock news. This hour program, as you will see, takes more than fifty people all day to produce.

On location, a camera operator films the governor of California on a visit to San Francisco.

When the camera operator returns to the station, he hands the film to a *film technician* who develops it using an automatic processing machine. Within an hour, the film will be ready for viewing.

Usually more film is shot than can be used on the air. A producer, working with a *film editor*, must select the best portion for use on the program.

The *environmental reporter* (background) and her writer-assistant (right) spend the day preparing information for the evening news. She will not only tell viewers about the day's weather and make a prediction for the following days, but will also explain some aspect of meteorology. She may, for example, explain how the jet stream affects the weather.

An editor puts the script for the news program together in proper order. Today's script is thirty-one pages long.

As six o'clock draws near, the *anchor*, who is the key member of the on-air news team, puts on his make-up. Make-up is needed because studio lights are so bright they make performers look unnaturally pale.

A technician loads pre-recorded videocassettes of TV commercials into a machine that will play them during breaks in the news.

The camera operators, electricians and other studio crew members prepare the equipment for the broadcast.

The camera operator sees what the camera sees by watching a tiny TV set called a *monitor* that is built into the camera.

The anchor and the environmental reporter get a very different view of what the studio looks like from what people at home see.

GOVERNOR BROWN
6 p.m.   5/16/78

SUB   3

JOHN LIVE:

SEVERAL TIMES SINCE
WE'VE BEEN DOING
THESE NEWSCENTER
FOUR/CALIFORNIA
POLLS, GOVERNOR
BROWN HAS BEEN IN
TOWN ON THE DAY WE
GOT THE RESULTS...

HE WAS HERE AGAIN
TODAY...SPEAKING TO
STUDENTS AT SAN
FRANCISCO STATE
UNIVERSITY...AND
WHEN WE SHOWED HIM
THESE LATEST RESULTS,
THE GOVERNOR ISSUED
YET ANOTHER PLEA
FOR SUPPORT FOR
PROPOSITION EIGHT...

TAKE FILM/SOUND UP FULL
TRT: 2A

ENDS: "...REALLY GET   ENDS: "...REALLY GET
A BARGAIN."   A BARGAIN."

Mounted on each camera is a *teleprompter* device that uses mirrors to project a copy of the script onto a pane of glass in front of the lens. The words are so close to the lens, the camera doesn't see them. This allows the anchor or other reporters on the set to read the script while looking directly into the camera.

Here's a portion of an actual script. The words on the left side of the page describe what the viewers see. The words on the right side are what the anchor or other studio reporters read.

The *floor manager* raises his hand to signal that the program is about to begin. This job includes coordinating all activity on the floor of the studio. The floor manager, in turn, receives directions over his earphones from the *program director* who is stationed in the control room.

In the *control room* the director and assistants guide the program. They choose what will go out over the air from twenty-two television screens. The screens show what each of the three studio cameras is seeing, plus news film, videotape, commercials and live reports—all ready to be played at the right moment.

The story about the governor's visit to town is on the air. The reporter spent all day on this story and was helped by half a dozen other people in its preparation. The story

now occupies just twenty-eight seconds of the one hour news program. And it is only one of several dozen stories that will be covered on this day.

Monopoly

Charles Darrow, the man who sold Monopoly to Parker Brothers.

After chess and checkers America's most popular board game is surely Monopoly, the Parker Brothers real estate trading game. The game was an instant hit when Parker Brothers released it in 1935. Since then, the game has become an American classic. Parker Brothers recently figured the company had "built" more than two and a half billion of the famous little green Monopoly houses in the last 40 years.

Parker Brothers' story about Monopoly's creation is one of those rags-to-riches tales that America is famous for. However, only a short while ago, a number of people came forward to dispute the Parker legend. The "inventor" of Monopoly, these people claim, never invented the game at all, but took a game which had been around for years, then sold it as his own. The question is still being argued, but here are both sides of the story:

In 1933, Parker Brothers says, Charles Darrow sat in his Germantown, Pennsylvania, kitchen. Like so many other people in the 1930s, Darrow had been thrown out of work by the Great Depression. Darrow had been a salesman of heating and engineering equipment. Now he was reduced to trying to sell handmade jigsaw puzzles to earn a few extra dollars. This particular night, he sat thinking of the good old days, when the family could afford to vacation in Atlantic City, New Jersey.

Darrow began sketching a game board on the piece of oilcloth that covered the kitchen table. He labeled game squares with the names of streets in Atlantic City—Baltic Avenue, Park Place, and Boardwalk. He used discarded bits of wood for houses and typed property cards on scrap cardboard. Darrow had created a new game which he named Monopoly.

The Darrow family played the game together. They enjoyed the feeling of becoming "millionaires" in the middle of the money-hungry depression. Soon they invited friends to their Monopoly nights. Many friends asked for copies of the game. Darrow made copies by hand and sold them for $4.00. Encouraged by his success, Darrow made some more sets which he offered to Philadelphia department stores. All the games sold. Darrow stepped up his production to meet the growing demand for Monopoly. By 1934 the demand was so great that Darrow could not handle it. He decided to sell his creation to a game company that could market Monopoly nationally. He chose Parker Brothers, one of the world's largest manufacturers of games.

Parker Brothers rejected the game immediately. They stated the game had "52 fundamental errors." In particular the company felt Monopoly was too long (a game

Elizabeth Magie Phillips, the unknown woman many people recognize as the true inventor of Monopoly.

was similar to Monopoly's. However instead of trying to own everything, players became "trust busters" trying to break up the monopolies on the board.

Now the law says that when a company invents a name for a product, it can register that name so that other people cannot use it on their own products. You cannot register a word that people are already using—like "orange juice"—but you can protect a new name—like "Orange Julius." So when Parker Brothers learned about Anti-Monopoly they accused Professor Anspach of violating their trademark. They claimed the name "Anti-Monopoly" sounded so much like "Monopoly" that customers would be confused. Anspach argued that no one would ever mix up the two names. When Parker Brothers sued, Anspach began a nationwide tour, appearing on radio and television to tell people about his problems with Parker Brothers.

Then came a temendous surprise. Someone called up the broadcasting station Anspach was appearing on one day and told the professor it did not matter whether or not the name "Anti-Monopoly" was too much like "Monopoly." This person said that Darrow could not have invented Monopoly in the 1930s because she had friends who had played the game years before that. More important, the name "Monopoly" was in widespread use so that Parker Brothers had no right to take the name for themselves in the first place.

Anspach immediately began to dig into the past. Eventually, he traced the origin of the game to a Virginia woman named Lizzie Magie. In Magie's time, ruthless business people were

should only last 45 minutes), and it did not have a definite goal (most of Parker's games started on one space and ended when players reached another; Monopoly players just kept going around the board). What's more, it was too complicated and confusing. Annoyed, Darrow went back to producing his own games. When two Philadelphia department stores ordered huge quantities for the Christmas season, Parker Brothers reconsidered. They offered to buy Darrow's game and give him a royalty on every set sold. Darrow accepted the offer. Parker Brothers published Monopoly in 1935 and had a hit on their hands. Charles Darrow retired a millionaire at age 46 and lived happily ever after. A plaque in his honor was erected in Atlantic City.

It is a nice story, the kind people like to hear. But in 1976 a San Francisco professor uncovered evidence that the familiar story of Monopoly's invention might not be true at all. The professor, Ralph Anspach, was being sued by Parker Brothers because of his new game, Anti-Monopoly. Anti-Monopoly's game board

Monopoly is serious business in a tournament. Two players intently study the board while a referee looks on.

buying up land to form huge monopolies. She felt these monopolies helped only the very rich, and therefore she created a game called The Landlord's Game to teach the evils of making money off land. In the Landlord's Game all players started equal, but by the end of the game one player had wiped the others out.

Though the Landlord's Game had different street names on the squares, the board and the rules were much like Monopoly. As people played Magie's game they began to make their own revisions. One of the biggest changes was allowing players to build houses and hotels on property. Around the same time, people started calling the game Monopoly. Players in different cities changed the property names to those of places in their own hometowns.

Eventually Monopoly was known in many parts of the eastern United States. Among the people who played the game was Dan Layman, who learned Monopoly at Williams College in 1927. Back home again in Indianapolis, Layman saw a chance to make some money with the game. Since he had not invented the game, he knew he could not patent it and he knew

he could not own the name. So he took the Monopoly rules, changed the board a little and called it Finance.

Soon after, one of Layman's friends taught Monopoly to his neighbor Ruth Hoskins, who later moved to Atlantic City. There she and her friends got the idea to name the properties after places in Atlantic city. This group of people used the famous Monopoly names we now know: Boardwalk, Park Place, the Reading Railroad and Marven Gardens. Yes, Marven Gardens, for that is the real name of the residential area after which the square was named.

From Atlantic City the game moved to Philadelphia, where a man named Todd played it. It was at one of the Todd Monopoly nights that Charles Darrow learned the game. Darrow was immediately interested and asked his host for a copy of the rules. Then he made a copy of the board. Soon Darrow was selling his own sets in Philadelphia. In 1935 he sold the game to Parker Brothers, pretending it was his own idea. Darrow told the company the story which the firm uses today as the origin of Monopoly.

Parker Brothers found out about the deception shortly thereafter, just as the game was becoming a national hit. Before Monopoly, the company had been having serious money problems. The new game helped save Parker Brothers' skin. If it came out that Monopoly were actually a thirty-year-old folk game, Parker Brothers could not patent it, and anybody could produce the game legally. Without a monopoly on Monopoly, Parker Brothers would never make the millions of dollars which stood just within reach. To avoid losing this bonanza, Parker Brothers quietly began to buy

Professor Ralph Anspach and his family playing Anti-Monopoly, the game that challenged Parker Brothers' monopoly of Monopoly.

facts. Of course, the original creators and their friends knew the real story. A few of them spoke out without result. Most said nothing. And some of the original Monopoly players were actually afraid to play on their old home-made game boards after Parker Brothers patented the game. They feared they might somehow be breaking the law!

So the story of the invention of the world's most popular board game seems to be more complicated than people have always thought. However, uncovering all this information did not help Professor Anspach. Parker Brothers officials did not contest the documents and the witnesses who told the story of Monopoly's early days. They simply said it did not matter who invented the game. People might buy Anti-Monopoly thinking it was a Parker Brothers game because of the name. The court agreed, and in mid-1977, 40,000 copies of Anti-Monopoly were ploughed into a Minnesota landfill. But Professor Anspach is still on the warpath. He is now putting out the identical game under the name "Anti." Another of his games, "Choice," revives the anti-monopolistic spirit of Lizzie Magie. Further, Anspach has appealed the trademark decision, hoping to break the Monopoly monopoly. Whether he will meet with success in the future nobody can tell.

But if there is doubt about the legal side of Monopoly, there is no doubt about the impact the game has had on America and the world. The trading game developed by the efforts of all those people, known and unknown, down through the years, continues to be a perennial favorite of game players everywhere.

up the rights to pre-Darrow versions of Monopoly. Lizzie Magie got $500 for her Landlord's Game. The company that had bought Finance from Dan Layman received $10,000 and agreed to keep quiet about its game. (Later Parker Brothers released another game called Finance, pretending it was a Monopoly imitation, instead of the other way around.) The final target was a Texan who produced his own Monopoly game called "Inflation." Parker Brothers sued him, but the man informed the court that Monopoly was an old game that could not be patented. Doing an about-face, Parker Brothers paid $10,000 to the Texan who then agreed to cooperate with Parker Brothers.

After that, a huge publicity campaign pushed Charles Darrow as the inventor of Monopoly. Even the biggest magazines were taken in, probably because the story sounded so believable, and nobody checked into the

The Early Days of Monopoly

Between the time Elizabeth Magie invented the Landlord's Game in 1904 and the present-day Monopoly was introduced in 1935, the game went through many forms. Monopoly was a "folkgame," that is, a game which was passed on by word of mouth from player to player, changing as it went along. Ralph Anspach's research has turned up some of the high points in the history of Monopoly.

The Landlord's Game

144   SPECIFICATIONS OF PATENTS—JANUARY 5, 1904.

adjacent ends, a sleeve-nut correspondingly screw-threaded engaging with said lining-tighteners, a compressible lining within said lining-tighteners, studs mounted in the body and engaging with said lining-tighteners to prevent them from turning, and a stud in a lining-tightener engaging with the lining and preventing it from turning, rotary movement of the lining and its tightener being thus prevented while longitudinal movement is permitted, substantially as set forth.

In witness whereof I have hereunto set my hand and seal, at Indianapolis, Indiana, this 21st day of June, A. D. 1901.

THOMAS J. LINDSAY. [L. S.]

Witnesses:
CHESTER BRADFORD,
L. H. COLVIN.

748,626. GAME-BOARD. Lizzie J. Magie, Brentwood, Md. Filed Mar. 23, 1903. Serial No. 149,177. (No model.)

To all whom it may concern:

Be it known that I, LIZZIE J. MAGIE, a citizen of the United States, residing at Brentwood, in the county of Prince George and State of Maryland, have invented certain new and useful improvements in Game-Boards, of which the following is a specification.

My invention, which I have designated "The landlord's game," relates to game-boards, and more particularly to games of chance.

The object of the game is to obtain as much wealth or money as possible, the player having the greatest amount of wealth at the end of the game after a certain predetermined number of circuits of the board have been made being the winner.

In the drawings forming a part of this specification, and in which like symbols of reference represent corresponding parts in the several views, Figure 1 is a plan view of the board, showing the various movable pieces used in the game; and Fig. 3 is a view of one of the boxes, the same being designated as the "bank."

The implements of the game consist of a board which is divided into a number of spaces or sections and four (4) spaces in the center indicating, respectively, "Bank," "Wages," "Public treasury," and "Railroad." Within these four spaces are preferably placed four (4) boxes, one of which is shown in the drawings and represented by the numeral 24.

The movable pieces used in the game, only one piece of each set for convenience of illustration being shown in the drawings, are as follows: Four pairs of dice, four shaking-boxes, four checkers to check the throws made, boxes representing, respectively,

"Bank," "Wages," "Public treasury," and "Railroad," and also various colored chips or tickets representing lots, money, deeds, notes, individual mortgages, bank mortgages, charters, legacies, and luxuries. These chips are not to be limited to any certain number or colors.

25 indicates lot tickets; 26, the dice; 27, shaking-boxes; 28, deeds; 29, notes; 30, individual mortgages; 31, bank mortgages; 32, charters; 33, luxuries; 35, money; 36, checkers, and 34 legacies.

The game is played as follows: Each player is provided with five hundred dollars. The lot tickets, twenty-two (22) in number, are placed face downward upon the board, and each player draws one until twelve have been taken. The rest are put back in the wages-box. Each player looks at the tickets he has drawn and may purchase the lot corresponding to his ticket if he can afford to or so chooses. If he does not purchase, he does not have to pay rent, but simply puts the ticket back into the wages-box again. When these twelve lots have been bought or the privilege refused and the owner's deeds placed upon those purchased, the game begins.

The series of spaces upon the board are colored to distinguish them; but of course other means of making them distinctive may be employed. The lot-spaces "1" to "22," which are preferably green, are for sale at the highest figure marked upon them or for rent at the lowest figure marked upon them. If a player chooses to buy a lot, he must pay into the "Public treasury" the price of it and place his deed upon it. If he chooses to rent it, he must pay the rent to the "Public treasury." (This represents indirect taxation.)

Absolute necessities: These spaces, which are preferably blue, indicate absolute necessities—such as bread, coal, shelter, and clothing—and when a player stops upon any of these he must pay five dollars into the "Public treasury." (This represents indirect taxation.)

No trespassing: Spaces marked "No trespassing" represent property held out of use, and when a player stops on one of these spaces he must go to jail and remain there until he throws a double or until he pays into the "Public treasury" a fine of fifty dollars. When he comes out, he must count from the space immediately in front of the jail.

Railroad: "R. R." represents transportation, and when a player stops upon one of these spaces he must pay five dollars to the "R. R." If a player throws a double, he "Gets a pass" and has the privilege of jumping once from one railroad to another, provided he would in his ordinary moving pass a "R. R." If he stops upon it, however, he must pay five dollars.

Luxuries: These spaces, preferably purple, represent the luxuries of life, and if a player stops on a "Luxury" he pays fifty dol-

Auction Monopoly

Elizabeth Magie patented her The Landlord's Game in January 1904, showing a copy of the board and a list of the rules. In Magie's game, there were no houses or hotels, and the properties were not in groups. However the play was much like Monopoly, and it had such features as railroads, utilities and a Go To Jail square. It was this game, never packaged commercially, that was passed along from person to person as a fun way to teach the evils of land monopoly.

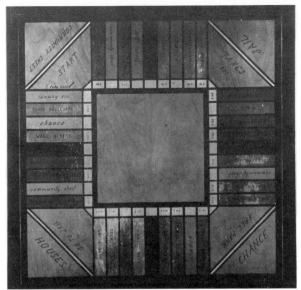

Here is a wooden Monopoly board, labeled with places such as Wall Street, Broadway, Chevy Chase, Grosse Point, and with joke names, such as Boomtown, Rickety Row, Easy Street.

This is the original oilcloth Monopoly board played by Ruth Hoskins and friends in Atlantic City in 1931.

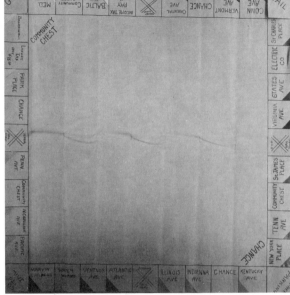

By 1910 the game had become Auction Monopoly. Auction Monopoly was probably invented by Guy Nearing of Arden, Delaware. His brother, Scott Nearing, took the game to the University of Pennsylvania, where he taught. Auction Monopoly spread rapidly, and by the 1920s was played in New York, Michigan, New Jersey, Texas, Pennsylvania, Massachusetts and Indiana.

Auction Monopoly introduced most of the remaining rules of present-day Monopoly. There were houses, property groups, Chance and Community Chest cards, and Free Parking. The main difference was that when a player landed on a piece of property, it was immediately put up for auction. (This still happens in modern Monopoly when a player chooses not to buy property he lands on.) The board (left) is a wooden Auction Monopoly board made in Royersford, Pennsylvania, about 1910. The place names come from the local area. Free Parking is a space which says, "Government Grant—no rents, no taxes. Rest in peace and depart."

When Parker Brothers learned of Lizzie Magie's The Landlord's Game, they bought out her patent. By the time Parker Brothers put the game out in the mid-1930s (above), the inventor was using her married name, Elizabeth Magie Phillips.

Atlantic City, Home of Monopoly

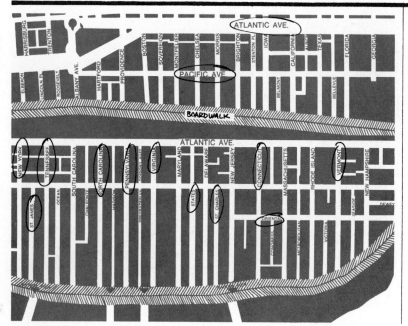

The familiar street names of the modern Monopoly were taken from places around Atlantic City, New Jersey. This map shows a section of Atlantic City from which many of the names were taken. The photographs are reproductions of postcards printed in Atlantic City during the 1910s and 1920s.

The Boardwalk

Marven Gardens

The La Fontaine hotel on Kentucky Avenue

Atlantic Avenue and the Reading
Railroad depot

New York Avenue

Pennsylvania Avenue

Tennessee Avenue and the Boardwalk

Galen Hall on Connecticut Avenue

Craig Hall, on Illinois Avenue

Pacific Avenue

The Clarendon Hotel, on Virginia Avenue

Monopoly Around the World

Today Monopoly is played throughout the world. Foreign editions are printed in many languages. Usually the property names on a foreign edition are changed to those of streets in the country's biggest city.

Monopoly for the blind is played on a standard board to which is glued a piece of molded plastic. Braille dots on the plastic identify the properties. Coded holes in the ridges surrounding each square tell the players which color group the property belongs to.

Title deeds are printed on large cards which carry the information both in print and in Braille dots. Money and Chance and Community Chest cards are made the same way. The game is played with special dice having one through six raised dots on each face.

Monopoly Trivia

So you think you know all about Monopoly? How many of these odd Monopoly facts do you know?

- The longest Monopoly game (with rotating teams of players) lasted 49 days or 1176 hours. The longest game with the same four players was 264 hours—eleven days and nights.

- The longest underwater game of Monopoly was 1008 hours or 42 days, played by rotating teams of scuba divers in a swimming pool. Their game equipment was specially made by Parker Brothers so the pieces would not float to the surface or fall apart. The special game cost $1500 to make.

- Other longest game records set by Monopoly fans—longest game played in a treehouse (123 hours); longest game in a moving elevator (288 hours); longest game underground (100 hours); longest game on a balance beam (also 100 hours, but this game had safety mats); longest anti-gravitational game (4 hours played on a ceiling); longest game on the back of a fire truck. (101 hours), and longest game in a bathtub (2 players—31 hours).

- The largest Monopoly game was a 550-foot-square outdoor game played at a Pennsylvania college (see page 112). The largest indoor game was set up in a Michigan shopping center in

Playing a game of Spanish Monopoly. The board is the same, but the money and the names of the properties are different. Here a player is about to land on "Suerte," the Spanish equivalent of "Chance."

Money in Spanish Monopoly is in the form of elaborate banknotes of different sizes, ranging in value from 100 to 10,000 pesetas. A player earns 20,000 pesetas for passing Go.

1972. The smallest Monopoly game was played on a board 1 inch square. That game lasted 15 hours.

In 1977 a World Monopoly Tournament was held in Monaco, the gambling capital of Europe. Players from all over the world were chosen by national elimination rounds. These players met in Monte Carlo for 5 hours of cut-throat play. The defending champion was John Mair, a 28-year-old banker from Ireland. The final round of play between the champions from Ireland, Britain, Germany, Italy and Singapore was transmitted to the crowd by closed-circuit TV. A play-by-play announcer covered the action. The game was won by Cheong Seng Kwa, a 31-year-old sales executive from Singapore. John Mair came in second. The winner's prize was a $5000 silver tray engraved with Monopoly symbols. The United States player made it to the fourth round, but did not place in the final.

- Monopoly was banned in the Soviet Union as being too "capitalistic." However Parker Brothers likes to think that underground Monopoly goes on in Russia, for all six Monopoly games displayed during the American National Exhibition in Moscow were stolen before the show ended.

- Computer analysis by Irvin Hetzel of Iowa State University has revealed the 10 squares most likely to be hit during a game of Monopoly. In order they are: Illinois Avenue, Go, B&O Railroad, Free Parking, Tennessee Avenue, New York Avenue, Reading Railroad, St. James Place, Water Works and Pennsylvania Railroad.

- Other analyses suggest that the worst investment in Monopoly are the Water Works and the Electric Company. The best investment is the orange property group: St. James Place, Tennessee Avenue and New York Avenue.

The Biggest Monopoly Game in the World

There have been many record-breaking Monopoly games, but none was quite like the game played at Juniata College. On April 29, 1967, a sunny Saturday, students of the Huntingdon, Pennsylvania college set the record for the world's biggest game of Monopoly.

The project was the brainchild of several Juniata seniors, led by William "Toby" Dills. Already experienced at other stunts and marathons, Dills and his friends decided to stage a huge outdoor Monopoly game with the freshman, sophomore, junior and senior classes as the four "players."

The board was laid out on campus sidewalks. It was about 550 feet square. The organizers painted the spaces with whitewash tinted with food coloring, expecting the mixture to wash off after the game was over. However, parts of the board were still visible a year later. Juniata students, shown on the Free Parking square, made houses, hotels, dice and other playing pieces. Money was cut from rolls of colored paper donated by a local newspaper. Property deeds, and Chance and Community Chest cards were lettered with Magic Markers on pieces of poster board. The houses and hotels were bookstore cartons painted with tempera paint.

The dice were 2-foot cubes stuffed with foam rubber, made by a local upholsterer. At first the students tossed the dice from the third-floor fire escape of the Students' Hall. After a few hours one die split open, and stuffing blew all over the lawn. The rollers repaired the die and moved their operation to the first floor. The giant dice were hauled back up in a volleyball net.

Each class built its own token. The senior class used a giant beer can made from an oil drum. With the can was a giant Liquor Control Board card to show the seniors were allowed to have the beer. The junior class used a Snoopy token and the sophomores a cardboard outhouse. The freshman token was an elaborate construction symbolizing the study of the humanities. The three columns represented the pillars of society: the whisky bottle and the noose were vice and punishment, the giant stuffed owl represented wisdom. Some students also thought it symbolic that "wisdom" got caught in a telephone wire on the first move and fell off.

As play progressed, the dice rolls, decisions to buy and other messages were relayed by two-way radio and bicycle. A local radio station carried play-by-play coverage of the game. After 7 hours, all the property had been purchased, though no team had a Monopoly. When the outdoor game was called off, the play moved indoors. The freshmen and sophomores had the upper hand, although no one was badly off. The junior class needed 6 hours to complete their first circuit of the board—they drew both Go To Jail cards, rolled three straight doubles several times and landed on the Go To Jail space. Just before the outdoor game ended the juniors and seniors joined forces.

How to Make Your Own Rules

Since the days when Monopoly was called The Landlord's Game, the rules of play have changed quite a bit. Though the official rules of Parker Brothers' version have remained the same since the 1930s, many Monopoly players have added their own rules to make the play livelier. You may already use some of these variations, or you may want to try them in your own Monopoly contests.

One of the most popular rule changes provides for a jackpot on the Free Parking space. In the official rules the square is simply a resting place (a nice spot to land when the board is lined with hotels). A player gets nothing for landing there. However, many players put money paid for taxes, Chance and Community Chest penalties and bail under the Free Parking corner. Any player to hit the space wins the accumualted cash. This money is called the "kitty," the "pot", or the "McGillicudy," depending where the game is played. Sometimes $500 is put in the kitty at the start of the game as a bonus for the first player to land on Free Parking.

Another popular rule takes away a player's "citizenship" when landing in jail. According to the offical rules, a player in jail may still collect rents and buy, sell or mortgage property. In the altered version, a jailed player cannot do any of these things until released from jail.

Still another variation of Monopoly permits players to make deals with each other for immunity from rent. ("I'll give you Park Place if you let me land on your property rent-free.") Another folk rule allows players to borrow money from each other. The official rules permit you to borrow only from the bank.

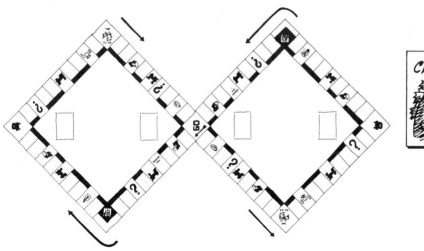

If regular Monopoly isn't complicated enough for you, try Double Monopoly. This requires two complete Monopoly sets. The boards are overlapped at the Free Parking squares. Play moves in a figure-8 pattern. In this version there are two Go spaces, so players collect a $400 salary during each circuit of the board. However in another Double Monopoly setup the first board's Free Parking space is covered by the second board's Go. In this game, once the houses start piling up, a player without a big cash reserve finds himself getting pretty low by the time rent for the two boards has been paid. In Double Monopoly all property is kept with the board on which it was bought. A player cannot combine one board's Baltic Avenue with the other board's Mediterranean to make a monopoly.

Another way to liven up your Monopoly game is to make your own Chance and Community Chest cards. Many players dissatisfied with the puny size of certain gifts ($10 for second prize in the beauty contest) make up for it with other cards ($100 for first prize). Some players prefer to pump up the "chance" element in the Chance cards with natural disasters— "Earthquake destroys all your houses." Others try for realism— "Your houses are condemned by the city. Tear them all down, or (a) pay $100 each for repairs, (b) pay the Bank a bribe of $1500." Of course, if you make one or two of your own cards, all the players will see the added card coming up in the deck and know what is in store. You could copy *all* the cards over so they all look the same, but that is too much trouble. A better idea is to create 6 or 7 cards for each stack. Shuffle them well. This way players will still know a special card is coming up, but they won't know which one it is.

MONTE CRISTO R.R.	AVENUE D	FIRST ST.	P.U.D. #1	AV
PRICE $200	PRICE $160	PRICE $140	PRICE $150	PR

You might also make a Monopoly game using streets in your own hometown. Which districts would be most appropriate for which squares? Where is your town's "Mediterranean Avenue?" Where is "Park Place?" If you don't have enough railroads to go around, use bus lines, taxicab companies or trucking firms. The Short Line in real Monopoly was actually named after an Atlantic City bus company, as only three railroads served the city. The squares above are from a Monopoly game based on places around the town of Snohomish, Washington.

King Kong

No movie creation has captured the world's imagination like King Kong, the monster ape that terrorized New York City before being shot off the top of the Empire State Building by guns from airplanes. Since his movie debut in 1933, King Kong has appeared in films, magazines, books, comics, TV commercials and a Saturday morning cartoon series. The ape has long since replaced Paul Bunyan as America's best-known folk hero. Whenever *King Kong* reappears on television, thousands of viewers twist the dial to see the familiar saga one more time.

Not bad for an ape less than two feet tall!

King Kong was the brainchild of a movie producer named Merian Cooper. He and his partner, Ernest Schoedsack, had led lives as exciting as those of the heroes of the film. The two met in 1918 during a war between Russia and Poland. Cooper was a fighter pilot who formed a squadron of Americans fighting with the Poles. Schoedsack was a cameraman who shot films of the war and did everything from driving ambulances to helping refugees escape. The men met again after the war. Cooper was a newspaper feature writer and Schoedsack was making newsreels, weekly roundups of world news which theaters showed in the days before television.

In those days, a lot of the world had yet to be explored. After World War I, a new age of expeditions and discovery began. In 1922, Cooper was hired as a writer for a seagoing expedition to Africa. The expedition needed a cameraman, so Cooper called on his friend Schoedsack. A partnership began which was to last throughout the two men's lives.

Soon the two adventure-lovers were shooting dramatic films in faraway places. In 1925 they filmed the migration of an Iranian tribe called the Bhaktiari. Cooper and Schoedsack were accompanied by Marguerite Harrison, an American author, on the tribe's gruelling trek across the mountains of Persia, now Iran. From this footage they made the feature film *Grass. Grass* was well-received by the critics but it did not make much money. Theater owners complained that the omission of stars and "love interest" limited their audiences.

Still, *Grass* did well enough to interest a big studio in giving Cooper and Schoedsack another chance. In the meantime, Ernest Schoedsack had served as cameraman for still another expedition. There he met Ruth Rose, a researcher whose life had been every bit as adventurous as his. Though she had started out as an actress, Ruth Rose joined the New York Zoological Society's research unit in British Guiana. She worked with all kinds of exotic animals, from jaguars to boa constrictors. Later she was made official historian of the expedition, and her articles were widely published. Schoedsack and Rose married just before a new movie expedition was to begin.

Over the next several years, the trio made movies in the jungles of Asia and the deserts of Africa. They shot footage under dangerous, almost impossible conditions. They braved bad weather and epidemics. They photographed elephant stampedes and tiger hunts. Out of this came *Chang*, a story of native life in Siam (now Thailand). The movie was a great success.

Meanwhile, Merian Cooper had become a big wheel in the new business of commercial aviation. He longed to go exploring again, but his responsibilities forced him to stay in New

Ernest Schoedsack (left) and Merian Cooper (right), the producers and directors of *King Kong.*

York. The Schoedsacks tried life in the big city as well, but their taste for adventure was too strong. Soon they were off to Sumatra to make another film. Cooper stayed home and dreamed of the old days. He haunted the National Geographic Society and the Explorer's Club. Finally, out of his longing for adventure came the germ of the idea for *King Kong.*

Cooper had read of the discovery of the "Komodo dragons," ten-foot-long lizards found only on a remote island in the South Pacific. Out of this came the notion of a giant prehistoric ape, discovered in an exotic land and transported to civilization. Then Cooper got the idea of the "Beauty and the Beast" theme, in which the ape would be captured and finally led to destruction by his love for a beautiful woman. Cooper wrote a proposal for his film, which he hoped would include an expedition to the island of Komodo. A few people were interested, but nobody was willing to put up the money for the project, which more than once was called "impossible." Reluctantly, Cooper shelved his plans.

Cooper did not know at that time that there was a man in the movie industry who could make the impossible possible. Willis O'Brien was a specialist in stop-motion animation, the process which made lifeless objects like rocks and furniture seem to move with a life of their own. Stop-motion had been known since the earliest days of movies. O'Brien had seen some of these early experiments during his days as a cartoonist, sculptor and prizefighter in California.

One day he was working in clay sculptures of boxers. His brother, who was helping him, began moving the arms on one sculpture, saying, "My boxer can beat yours!" This gave O'Brien the idea to animate his sculptures for short films. Soon he had made many trick films. Often they featured prehistoric life, O'Brien's favorite subject. Because of his efforts he was hired by First National Pictures in 1925 for the production of *The Lost World*, a fantasy film about explorers who capture a dinosaur and take it to London.

With the help of a young sculptor named Marcel Delgado, O'Brien created an amazing group of miniature dinosaurs, complete with their own tiny land. The results were impressive. In fact, they were so impressive that Sir Arthur Conan Doyle, author of the book on which the movie was based, used O'Brien's test films to play a trick on some old rivals.

Doyle, best known as the creator of Sher-

lock Holmes, was a strong believer in ghosts and spiritualism. For a long time professional magicians had made fun of his beliefs, saying that Doyle had been taken in by cheap tricks. Harry Houdini, a famous magician and escape artist, invited Doyle to a magician's convention in New York. Doyle agreed to attend. After the magicians had displayed their best tricks, Doyle announced that he had a trick of his own. Without explanation, he screened a reel of O'Brien's animated dinosaurs. Though ani-mated films weren't new, nothing as realistic as this had ever been seen before. The magi-cians were mystified. Next day, the *New York Times* wondered whether the beasts on the film were real. Doyle had topped the magicians' greatest stunts, and O'Brien's miniature mon-sters had won the seal of approval.

The Last World was a great success. O'Brien should have been set in his career. Unfor-tunately, however, none of his later projects ever seemed to work out. Then, in 1929, "talking pictures" set the movie industry on its ear. Many studios were put out of business when they could not adapt to the new medium fast enough. The difficulties of working with early sound equipment made it very hard to make movies out of doors or to film action that had been possible during the silent days. For awhile, just having sound guaranteed a picture's success with the public. Adventure pictures were replaced by films of people standing around talking to each other in the manner of the theater. Many of the complicated projects left over from the silent days were dropped.

In another way, 1929 was a bad year. The stock market crash that year brought on the Great Depression. Money became scarce. Many studios closed their doors forever. Producers in the surviving companies became very careful with their dollars. The depression put an end to many peoples' dreams. But surprisingly, hard times were going to make Merian Cooper's dreams come true.

Sometimes it seems as though "fate" takes a hand in the creation of masterpieces. All the right people come together in the right place at the right time; all the necessary events take place just when they should, and something great is created. This is certainly what happened with King Kong.

RKO, one of the newer movie studios, was on the verge of going broke in 1932. Its new manager, David Selznick, had orders to trim off the fat and keep the company afloat. Selznick needed somebody to help him decide which of RKO's unfinished movies ought to be completed and which should be scrapped. He hired Merian Cooper for the job.

It so happened that Willis O'Brien and Maurice Delgado were working for RKO putting together a movie called *Creation*, the idea of a fine movie director named Harry Hoyt. *Creation* was the story of shipwrecked explorers who find an island of prehistoric animals. The movie was already costing too much and probably would never be finished. But when Cooper saw the footage of O'Brien's animated prehistoric world, he knew he had at last found a chance to realize his giant gorilla story. He talked the project over with O'Brien and Selznick. Both were interested, and King Kong was born. Cooper called his old friend Ernest Schoedsack in to help with the picture.

People think that movies, like books, are usually written by one person. This isn't always the case. King Kong had three main writers before the movie was finished. The first, Edgar Wallace (a popular English thriller writer), died before he could do any important work on the film. The second, James Creelman, came up with many good ideas, but simply could not produce a script that satisfied Cooper and Schoedsack. Finally Schoedsack asked his wife to write the script. He could not have made a better choice. Combining her own ideas with those of Creelman, Schoedsack and Cooper, and then drawing upon her own background in exploration, Ruth Rose polished the story and the dialogue which were so important to King Kong's success.

The problems encountered in filming the story of King Kong, Eighth Wonder of the World, seemed almost too numerous to solve. Virtually everyone who heard about the project predicted it would fail. Yet Willis

When *King Kong* was still in the idea stage, artists made drawings of dramatic scenes for the proposed film. These were used as guides for action and set building. Above is a drawing of Kong fighting a tyrannosaur done by Byron Crabbe. Below, Mario Larrinaga depicts Kong fighting the snake lizard inside his cave.

O'Brien and his technical wizards met every challenge. Old processes were refined, and whole new ones invented to perform camera miracles. The impact of the pioneering special effects work done for *King Kong* is still felt in making movies today.

The combination of an imaginative story, excellent script, good acting and convincing staging made *King Kong* an immediate success when it opened in 1933. Audiences throughout the world thrilled to the capture of the giant ape and mourned Kong's death by the guns of airplanes. The film saved RKO from bankruptcy and started Schoedsack and Cooper on long, productive careers. *King Kong* was re-released many times through the years, each time finding a new audience. A sequel, *Son of Kong*, was released the next year. There were many imitations and spin-offs, but none came close to matching the popularity of the greatest ape of them all. *King Kong* has become a movie classic.

The Story of King Kong

Documentary filmmaker Carl Denham (played by Robert Armstrong) brings his crew to Skull Island, intending to capture on film the mysterious Kong, god of the island natives. With him is Ann Driscoll (Fay Wray), whose job it will be to add "love interest" to the film.

The local natives are about to give a tribeswoman to Kong as a sacrificial gift. When they see Ann, they decide she would make a much better present. The natives kidnap Ann that night and tie her to a special altar beyond the Great Wall that was built to keep Kong from their village.

Kong accepts his unwilling gift and
disappears into the forest. Denham
and his first mate Jack Driscoll
(Bruce Cabot) discover what has
happened. They lead the film crew
in pursuit of Kong. The land beyond the Great Wall is a prehistoric
jungle, and most of the film crew
die in combat with huge dinosaurs.
Meanwhile Kong has trouble of his
own. Ann almost escapes her
captor while the ape battles a tyrannosaur. However Kong recaptures
her and takes Ann to his mountain-
top lair. While the ape is fighting
another monster, Jack rescues Ann,
and the two make a daring escape
down a river.
The chase resumes, this time with
Kong the pursuer. He breaks down
the gate in the Great Wall and
destroys the native village. Denham's
crew overcomes the monster ape
with sleeping gas. The filmmaker
decides to take Kong back to
New York and make a lot of money
displaying him.

KING KONG

Kong is chained on a theater stage. Photographers begin taking flash pictures, and the ape thinks they are attacking Ann. His love for the girl is so great, Kong finds the strength to break free. The audience panics and Kong goes on a rampage. Jack hides Ann in a nearby hotel. But Kong turns the city upside down hunting for her, knocking over an elevated train and trampling passersby.

At last Kong locates Ann. By this time the greatest ape-hunt in history is under way. Kong flees, girl in hand, to the top of the Empire State Building. Suddenly, Navy fighter planes appear and begin firing at the ape. King Kong is doomed, but he puts Ann on a ledge before falling to his death in the street below. Minutes later, Jack reaches her and pulls her to safety.

Carl Denham stands by the great ape's body. A policeman says, "Well, Mr. Denham, the airplanes got him."

"No," replies Denham, "it wasn't the airplanes. It was *beauty* killed the beast!"

Who Was King Kong?

Kong and his keeper. Special effects man Buz Gibson makes Kong climb the model of the Empire State Building.

Fay Wray, placed atop a tree, recoils from her captor. The tree was a full-size mock-up. The animated Kong was projected onto a giant screen behind the tree (rear-screen projection is explained in greater detail on page 128).

Even today the story makes the rounds that King Kong was an actor in an ape suit. At least two actors have claimed to be the "man inside Kong." This simply is not true. Much of the misinformation came from magazine articles printed at the time *King Kong* was released, written by people who did not know what they were talking about. Animation is so familiar today that it is hard to remember how unique Kong was in 1933. Nobody had seen anything like it, and the King Kong miniatures were so realistic that many people were convinced they were the actual thing.

The real King Kong was a model eighteen inches tall. Over a movable metal skeleton was a layer of rubber which, in turn, was covered with rabbit fur. King Kong was made to "live" on screen by filming his movements one frame at a time. Between each frame an animator moved the Kong model a tiny bit. When the film was projected at normal speed, Kong seemed to move by himself. The detailed miniature jungles and buildings completed the effect.

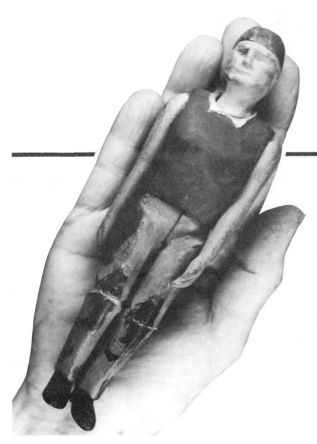

There were six Kong models. The spares were made because the wear and tear of animation would have worn out a single model. If you look closely at some scenes in *King Kong*, you will see that Kong's fur seems to "bristle," as if blown by a breeze. The "bristling" is the effect of the animator's fingers disturbing the model's fur as King Kong is moved between shots.

Three features of King Kong's body were made full size. A monstrous head and shoulders were built for close-ups of Kong's face. The head was made over a skeleton of wood and metal, covered with rubber and bearskins. The nose alone was two feet across. Kong's giant face could be moved to create different expressions. Another full-size feature was the giant mechanical hand built to hold live actors. A metal armature was padded with sponge rubber and covered with realistic fur and skin. The final full-size feature was a giant foot which is seen close up stepping on a dinosaur and trampling people as Kong rampages through a native village.

Left, many scenes in *King Kong* called for the ape to pick up or chase real people. For these scenes, the movie-makers used tiny wooden people like the half-finished one above. Close shots would show the live actor reacting to the ape, then a long shot would show Kong lifting a "struggling" miniature.

Right, in this long shot of the tyrannosaur scene, Fay Wray's "double" is a wooden miniature.

Part of the miniature New York City built for Kong's escape scene. The trolley car is only about 10 inches high. In this shot you can see the holes in the "ground" which fitted pegs in Kong's feet and kept the model upright. The holes were hidden by camera angles in the finished film.

Kong fights the airplanes. The Kong miniature stands atop a model of the Empire State Building as model planes swoop down on invisible wires. The city stretching into the distance is actually a flat painting. The airplane in the background seems to be far away; in reality it is a very small model hanging only a little ways from the larger foreground plane.

Building the giant head used for close-ups of Kong's face.

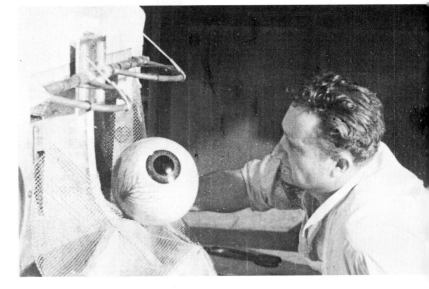

Each of Kong's wood-and-plaster eyeballs was as big as a bowling ball.

How to be a Movie Magician

Sometimes filmmakers are faced with a peculiar problem. They must take movies of something that doesn't exist! In fantasy movies like *King Kong*, almost nothing but the actors is real. The rest—Kong himself, Skull Island, the Great Wall, the S. S. *Venture*—never really existed. To make the unreal seem real is the job of the *special effects technician*.

Using film tricks like *process photography*, special effects experts can bring a prehistoric jungle to life or put an actor into a scene shot a thousand miles away. Here are simplified explanations of some of the camera magic to be found in the effects expert's bag of tricks.

Rear-Screen Projection

Problem: your script calls for a shot of the hero leaning on the rail of a ship, looking at a tropical island. It would be far too expensive to haul the actor and an entire camera crew to the South Pacific for that one shot. As the special effects technician, you may decide to use a process shot called *rear-screen projection*.

First you find some film of a tropical island. You may be given footage shot especially for the occasion, or you may find what you want in the library of *stock footage*—a file of shots of assorted locales and action which may be used over and over.

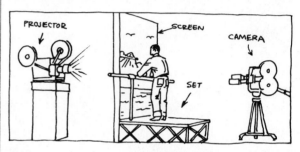

Now you build a simple set with a ship's rail. Behind the rail is a special movie screen. When a movie projector is directed at the screen from behind, the picture will show through. A camera records the combination of the set and the screen.

In the final film the actor appears to be aboard a ship looking at the distant island. Rear projection is not used as often as it was in the past because the background scene often looks fuzzy, or a different color from the live action.

There are several rear-projection shots in *King Kong*. One is the scene in which the rescue party "walks past" a rear-projected dying dinosaur.

Glass Shot

Problem: the script specifies a shot of two actors standing in the middle of a huge jungle. Going to a real jungle is out of the question, and your studio hasn't the space to build a full-size fake one. This might be a good time to use a *glass shot.*

You build a jungle set just big enough to handle the action. If your actors are simply going to stand and talk, you might need a set only a few feet square.

On a plate of glass, an artist paints a realistic picture of a jungle. A clear spot is left in the painting where the live action will appear. The artist is careful to match as closely as he can the color, shadows, etc., of the original set.

The glass painting is placed in front of the camera facing the set. The glass is lined up so that the trees and foliage in the set match the details of those in the picture. In the completed shot, the characters seem to be standing in a vast jungle.

There are many uses of glass painting in *King Kong.* One is the shot of the beach of Skull Island. The beach is a real California beach, but the rest of the island is a realistic painting.

Mirror Shot

Problem: you want to show an actor standing in the doorway of a castle, speaking to someone in the window overhead. Unfortunately, there are no castles in Burbank, and the producer refuses to build one. You might decide to use a *mirror shot,* sometimes called the *Schufftan process* after the man who invented it.

The castle is a detailed scale model built on a table-top. All the necessary backdrops, foreground shrubbery and the like are part of the model.

The only things you build full size are the doorway and the window where the actors will appear. The details in the full-scale set (like brickwork) correspond to those in the model.

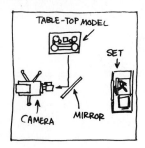

The camera is set up facing the set. In front of it is a mirror at a forty-five degree angle. The mirror reflects an image of the model castle. You scrape away the reflective part of the mirror in the spots where the action will appear, the door and the window. Now there are two "holes" in the mirror image. . .

. . .through which the full-sized set will show. In the completed shot, the actors seem to be standing in the model castle.

King Kong uses no mirror shots, but the device was popular at the time this movie was made. Since then, it has been largely replaced by matte photography (explained later on).

Miniature Projection

Problem: you need a scene in which an actor, hiding in a shallow cave, is menaced by a monster. The cave and the monster are both miniatures, though, and the actor does not want to be shrunk to six inches in height. What

do you do? You might use a variation of rear-screen projection called *miniature projection*.

First, you film the actor reacting to the monster.

Then you build the miniature set. As you do, you put a tiny movie screen in the back of the cave where the actor is to be hiding. Then you load a projector with the live action footage and aim it at the movie screen. As you film the animated monster frame by frame, you also project the live footage one frame at a time.

In the completed shot, the actor will appear in the cave, seemingly right there in the miniature along with the monster. Miniature projection was used often in *King Kong*, not only in the scenes in Kong's cave, but also in the final scene, in which Fay Wray was projected onto the model of the top of the Empire State Building.

Traveling-Matte Photography

Problem: the hero is to be in the foreground, yelling as the monster approaches him. You could do this with rear-screen projection, but as we noted earlier, it often isn't convincing. Instead, you might choose to use *traveling-matte photography*, a complicated but very useful process which allows you to do things none of the other methods will.

First you shoot your animated monster in his miniature background.

Now you film the live action. The hero stands in a jungle set, facing a special backing screen. Many types of screens are used in different matte processes. One popular type is a brilliant blue.

A special copy is made of the live action film, and the original saved for later.

The "special copy" of the live action is made by a complex developing method. All the parts of the picture where the blue screen showed through come out clear. All the parts where the screen was blocked by the set or the actor come out black. You now have a "mask" of the live action.

You combine the mask with the animated footage in a machine called an *optical printer*. The combined footage will show the animated monster, but everywhere the mask covered the animated footage there is now a transparent "hole" the same shape as the live action. Now you can take the original live action footage and match it up with the new copy. The live action will show through the holes.

The finished footage shows the hero being frightened by the approaching monster, just as you wanted.

You must be careful when lining up the two halves of a matte shot. If the pieces are slightly out of line, it will show on the screen. If you have seen a lot of movies, you have probably noticed what happens when the pieces do not line up. The mismatch shows as a blue or green halo around the actor. This is called a *fringe*. Fringing is much more common in movies made before the late 1960s. Advances in matte processes have made alignment much more accurate in today's films.

Matte shots are used throughout *King Kong*. Just one example is Kong's appearance in the door of the Great Wall before he attacks the native village. The wall and the village were a full-sized set, and Kong's image was *matted in* to the scene.

How to Make a Movie

Even though you may not have the thousands of dollars and the team of technicians it took to make a move like *King Kong*, you can still have fun shooting your own movie stories. You can make simple movies with a camera, some film and a handful of friends for actors. Here's how to do it:

1. *Write a script.*

The best movies are planned on paper. If you try to make up your story as you go along, the results are almost sure to be confusing and amateurish. Take the time to write a *script.* Your script doesn't have to be fancy. The main thing is to break up the action into separate parts. This is because movie stories are told bit by bit much the same way comic strip stories are.

The simplest script can be nothing more than a list of the bits of action. Filmmakers call each bit a *shot.* The *subject* of the shot is what the viewers will see on the screen—someone running, a gun, a flying saucer, etc. Usually the script tells how close the subject is to the camera. In a *long shot* the subject will seem to be far away, and much of the surrounding background will be visible. In the *close-up*, on the other hand, the subject is very close. A *close-up* might show only a person's face. Between these extremes is the *medium shot.*

The type of shot you choose for a bit of action makes a big difference in the way the story appears to the viewer. To help planning shots, many filmmakers, especially those making animated films, prepare their script in the form of a *storyboard.* The storyboard is a sort of silent comic strip in which every shot is represented by a sketch with a description of the action written underneath. Turn the page for three action scenes to go with the script on the next page.

Note that there are only sixteen action shots in our script. While Hollywood movies have hundreds and hundreds of shots, it's best to make your first few films much shorter than that. Also, this script is for a silent movie. The whole story is told by the actions of the actors. Silent movies are easier to make, and you can probably get better results since it is often hard to get clear sound using amateur equipment. It would be possible,

Sample Movie Script

Only a Dream

1. (Long shot) The hero appears around the corner of a building and comes running toward the camera. A few seconds later someone (some thing) comes around the same corner obviously chasing the hero.

2. (Close up) The hero gives a frightened look backward.

3. (Close up) We see the weird awful face of the monster who is chasing the hero.

4. (Long shot) We see the monster chasing the hero.

5. (Long shot) We see the hero turn down another street.

6. (Close up) We see the hero scream.

7. (Medium shot) We see a second monster coming from the opposite direction.

8. (Medium shot) We see the hero turn around.

9. (Medium shot) We see the first monster appear.

10. (Close up) The hero screams again.

11. (Medium shot) We see the hero tossing and turning in bed.

12. (Close up) The hero rubs both eyes and opens them.

13. (Medium shot) From behind we see someone trying to comfort the hero.

14. (Close up) The hero looks up at the comforter.

15. (Close up) The comforter turns out to be one of the monsters.

16. (Close up) Again the hero screams.

17. The end.

② CLOSE-UP HERO'S FACE —

③ CLOSE-UP MONSTER

④ LONG SHOT FROM
WINDOW — MONSTER
CHASES HERO

of course, to tell the audience what the actors are saying by including *title cards* the way old-time movies used to do it.

2. *Cast the movie*

Figure out who you want to play each part. You will probably find that friends, relatives and neighbors will all enjoy being movie stars.

3. *Scout your locations.*

Figure out where you will shoot each scene.

4. *Gather your props.*

If your script calls for a ray gun or a robot, gather such things before you start shooting.

5. *Create your titles.*

There are many ways to get titles. You can print them on cards, write them on blackboards, spell them out with objects, etc. If you want to add dialog to a silent film, the usual way is to use white lettering on a dark card—it is easier to read.

6. *Rehearse each bit of the action.*

You will save film if your actors know exactly what they should do each time the camera is turned on.

"Help!
Please, someone,
HELP ME!"

7. *Hold the camera steady when shooting.*

The worst mistake amateurs make is to jiggle the camera or move it around too much. Let the actors provide the motion. For best results, put the camera on a tripod. The only time it really makes sense to pan the camera (to move it) is when you are following some action—an actor who is running or a car that is moving.

8. *Make sure there is enough light.*

Read the directions in the film box and your camera's operating manual for this. Some cameras adjust to the light by themselves, but if yours must be adjusted by hand, be sure to check the setting each time the light changes. For instance, a camera set for a shot in an open, sunny field will not be set right for a shot in a dark alleyway.

9. *Edit the film.*

After your film is developed, you can always cut out bad parts and even switch pieces of the action around. Professional filmmakers spend a lot of time cutting apart and reassembling (*splicing*) the film. You probably won't want to do too much of that since super 8mm film is hard to work with. Too many splices can cause problems when you project the finished movie. You can find books about editing film at your local camera store or at the library.

KING KONG

How to Make a Flip-Book

How do movies move? You have probably seen that a movie film is made up of hundreds of tiny still pictures, each a little different from the one before. A projector flashes these pictures on the screen so fast that the viewers cannot see individual frames. Instead they get the impression that they are watching continuous motion.

You can put this principle of movement to work by making a *flip book*. Get a tablet, a stack of paper or a cast-off book. Near the edge of the last page, make a simple drawing

like a ball or square. Then flip down the next page. Repeat the drawing, a little to one side of the first. Keep doing this on each page, moving the position of the drawing a little each time. If you flip through the pages with your thumb, the drawings will seem to move from one side of the page to the other!

Once you have practiced with simple figures, try something harder, like stick people. Make arms and legs move by drawing everything the same as in the previous drawing, except for the moving parts. The greater the distance between one step of the movement and the next, the faster the arms or legs will seem to move.

To see how a flip book works, try the one below. Make a photocopy of the pages, then

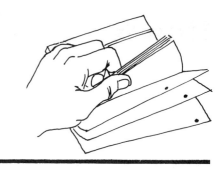

cut out each drawing. Paste each drawing on a page of a tablet, starting with the bottom page. Use the corner marks to line up the drawings with the corner of the page. Now flip through the pages and see why "'Twas Buick killed the beast!"

How to Do Stop-Motion Animation

Stop-motion animation applies the flip-book principle to movies. An inanimate object can be brought to life by filming it one frame at a time, moving the object a little bit between each frame. This is the way King Kong moved. Here's how to get started doing your own stop-motion animation.

You will need a movie camera, some film, a tripod, a cable release, and if you are filming indoors, some movie lights. The camera should be able to take one frame at a time. If yours cannot, practice pushing the release very quickly, letting no more than two or three frames go by. Animation done in this way will be a little jerky, but you can still get fair results. Mount the camera on a tripod. The tripod ensures that the camera does not move while you're adjusting your subject. The cable release, which screws into the shutter switch of the camera, lets you make your exposures without jiggling the camera.

For your first animation project, use a simple object like a toy car.

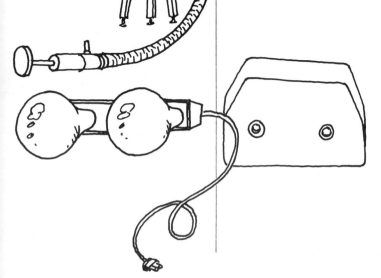

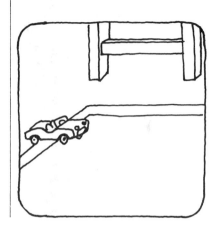

Set your camera on its tripod so that the car appears at one side of the viewfinder. Be sure you have enough light for filming.

To begin with, try making the car "drive" from one side of the screen to the other. Take several frames of the car in its original position. Press the cable release gently and take care not to bump the camera or the lights.

Now begin moving the car, a little bit at a time. Each time you move it, take one or two frames. Two frames each time will smooth out the motion on screen. The farther you move the car between shots, the faster it will seem to move in the finished movie.

But be careful! A movie projector shows either 18 frames (silent) or 24 frames (sound) every *second*. The most common mistake of beginning animators is moving the subject too much between frames. In the finished film, the car shoots across the screen, and the whole thing is over almost before it starts.

To avoid this problem, decide how long you want the scene to last by acting it out first while timing it. Multiply the number of seconds the action should take by 18. This tells you how many frames to shoot. For the action to last 5 seconds you will need to shoot 5 × 18 or 90 frames.

You can invent endless variations on simple animation. You might want your car to drive up a table leg.

Just stick a lump of clay to the bottom of the car. Then stick the car to the table leg.

Film the scene at an angle from which the clay does not show. Move the car a little higher each time you shoot. It will seem to climb up the table leg.

You can also animate furniture, books, balls—just about anything. Perhaps you will want your car to chase a chair around the room.

After a bit of practice, you will be ready to try more complex animation, such as animating figures. Most baby dolls are not flexible enough to be animated well, but "adventure dolls" like "G.I. Joe" are great for movie use.

Move the arms and legs of the doll a little at a time, as you did the car. You can add to your scenes cars, plane models, monsters—anything you can think of.

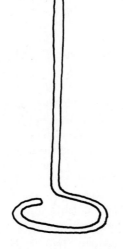

One problem with dolls is that they tend to fall over when you try to make them "walk." A stiff wire stand will hold the doll upright. Be sure that you shoot from an angle where the stand does not show. A more difficult but more effective way to keep the model on its feet is to attach pegs to the doll's feet. Then drill holes in a piece of wood to use as a "ground." To hold the doll in position, fit the pegs into the holes. This was how animators kept King Kong standing up.

Flexible plastic figures like "Gumby" toys are also useful for animation. A wire skeleton inside the figure holds it in any position you put it. Many superheroes and villains are available as flexible toys.

CLAY

Rubber spiders make a fun scary subject, though they are harder to animate (you have eight legs to worry about). Little bits of clay will hold the legs in place.

To build a miniature world for your creations to move around

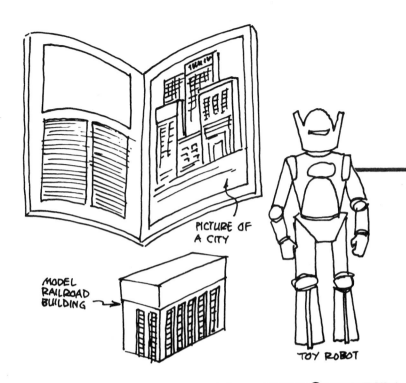

PICTURE OF A CITY

MODEL RAILROAD BUILDING

TOY ROBOT

When the miniature is filmed, the robot seems to be standing in the middle of the city.

There is almost no limit to what you can do with animation. All you really need is imagination. And patience! It takes a long time to film animation. You can speed things up by working with an animation team. One person can operate the camera, one can move the models, others can take care of lights and backgrounds. Just be sure all team members are out of camera range before you trip the shutter; otherwise your miniatures will suddenly be menaced by a giant human hand!

in, use houses, trees and buildings made for model train sets. For backgrounds you can use cut-outs from magazines. For example, use a toy robot, some plastic buildings and a photo of a city cut from a travel magazine.

The photo is pasted to a stiff cardboard backing. In front of the photo we put the robot, and in front of him the toy buildings.

Levi's

Levi Strauss, as he appeared during the Gold Rush in the 1850s.

Of all those who caught California gold fever in 1849, none cured it in a more unexpected way than Levi Strauss.

Strauss had come to America from Germany only a few years earlier. But when he learned about the fabulous gold strike at Sutter's mill, he was ready to explore another new frontier. He was just twenty years old when he boarded a ship in New York bound for California by way of Cape Horn. To raise money for his grubstake, he intended to sell the bundles of cloth he had brought from his brothers' shop.

By the time he reached San Francisco early in 1850, the would-be prospector had sold all his goods to his shipmates except for a roll of canvas cloth. This he expected to sell either to a tentmaker or to someone who needed a new top for a covered wagon.

That was his plan, but it was not how things worked out. One of the first San Franciscans Levi Strauss met when he left the ship was a miner who asked whether the new arrival had brought any pants with him from the East Coast.

Why pants? wondered Levi.

The miner explained that prospecting was such tough work, gold seekers quickly wore out their trousers. Thus, there was a shortage of hard-wearing pants.

A lot of newcomers must have heard the same story and probably shrugged it off. Not Levi Strauss. It turned out Strauss was more merchant than miner. He saw a need. He saw a way to meet it. All he had to do was make a pair of pants out of his roll of tough canvas. Strauss did it, and his customer loved them. The miner bragged about them to his friends. Soon people all over the gold country wanted the same kind of pants for themselves. Levi urgently asked his brothers to send out more canvas. His thoughts moved from gold to pants. But as it turned out, in terms of wealth there wasn't much difference.

Who actually cut the first pair of pants that became the model for the millions of pairs to follow? Some people say it was Levi Strauss himself. Others claim Levi simply hired some unknown and unsung tailor. No one knows for certain because the Levi Strauss Company's records were destroyed in the famous 1906 San Francisco earthquake.

But one thing is sure: Levi Strauss got the credit. While he always insisted on calling his product "pantaloons" or "overalls," the miners who bought them called them "Levi's" from the beginning. The name has remained unchanged for over a century and so has the basic design of the pants—snug, low on the hips, tapering on the legs. While the company in recent years has added new styles, there have been only two major changes in the basic Levi's pants since the beginning.

The first was the gradual shift from canvas cloth to the somewhat lighter but also very durable material called *denim*. Denim in those days came mainly from the town of Nimes, France. Named for the French words *de Nimes* meaning simply "from Nimes," it was made from cotton threads woven in a twill pattern—each crossing thread going under two threads and then over the next two. This produces the well-known diagonal pattern of the cloth. Other clothes makers had used denim before. But Levi Strauss was the first to color it dark blue using indigo dye. The dark color made it easier to match pieces of cloth and somehow it seemed perfect for the style. Before long, blue denim was the most famous pants material in the world. (In case you're wondering, "blue jeans" are the same as "blue denims." The word "jeans" comes from Genoa, the town in Italy where Columbus was born. Apparently, twill was manufactured in Genoa just as it was in Nimes.)

Levi Strauss was lucky when it came to miners. The second major development in Levi's is said to have taken place because of a miner named Alkali Ike. Ike had a habit of carrying ore samples in the back pockets of his Levi's. Unfortunately, the weight of the rocks would tear the seams. Ike kept complaining to his tailor Jake Davis that there ought to be a way to make the pockets stronger. Almost as a joke, the tailor took Ike's pants to the local blacksmith and had the rear pockets riveted into position. Joke or no joke, Ike was delighted with the repair job. Months later, his back pockets were still as good as new.

Davis eventually told Levi Strauss about his invention, and the two men joined forces. The tailor patented the riveting process, and Strauss hired him to be foreman of his factory. For the next several decades, Levi's were the only pants with rivets in the world, and their fame spread among miners.

Still, if Levi's had remained a uniform only for gold seekers, the pants probably would have been long forgotten. Eventually the gold ran out. But during the 1860s, overland traders brought news of the Levi's to the southwest and especially to Texas. There, cowboys who worked as hard as miners found that the pants could take the wear and tear of horseback riding and cattle driving and were comfortable as well. Soon Levi's were the only pants a self-respecting cowboy would wear. And

The first customers for Levi's pants were California gold miners.

JACOB W. DAVIS, OF RENO, NEVADA, ASSIGNOR TO HIMSELF AND LEVI STRAUSS & COMPANY, OF SAN FRANCISCO, CALIFORNIA.

IMPROVEMENT IN FASTENING POCKET-OPENINGS.

Specification forming part of Letters Patent No. **139,121**, dated May 20, 1873; application filed August 9, 1872.

To all whom it may concern :

Be it known that I, JACOB W. DAVIS, of Reno, county of Washoe and State of Nevada, have invented an Improvement in Fastening Seams; and I do hereby declare the following description and accompanying drawing are sufficient to enable any person skilled in the art or science to which it most nearly appertains to make and use my said invention or improvement without further invention or experiment.

My invention relates to a fastening for pocket-openings, whereby the sewed seams are prevented from ripping or starting from frequent pressure or strain thereon; and it consists in the employment of a metal rivet or eyelet at each edge of the pocket-opening, to prevent the ripping of the seam at those points. The rivet or eyelet is so fastened in the seam as to bind the two parts of cloth which the seam unites together, so that it shall prevent the strain or pressure from coming upon the thread with which the seam is sewed.

In order to more fully illustrate and explain my invention, reference is had to the accompanying drawing, in which my invention is represented as applied to the pockets of a pair of pants.

Figure 1 is a view of my invention as applied to pants.

A is the side seam in a pair of pants, drawers, or other article of wearing apparel, which terminates at the pockets; and *b b* represent the rivets at each edge of the pocket opening. The seams are usually ripped or started by the placing of the hands in the pockets and the consequent pressure or strain upon them. To strengthen this part I employ a rivet, eyelet, or other equivalent metal stud, *b*, which I pass through a hole at the end of the seam, so as to bind the two parts of cloth together, and then head it down upon both sides so as to firmly unite the two parts. When rivets which already have one head are used, it is only necessary to head the opposite end, and a washer can be interposed, if desired, in the usual way. By this means I avoid a large amount of trouble in mending portions of seams which are subjected to constant strain.

I am aware that rivets have been used for securing seams in shoes, as shown in the patents to Geo. Houghton, No. 64,015, April 23, 1867, and to L. K. Washburn, No. 123,313, January 30, 1872; and hence I do not claim, broadly, fastening of seams by means of rivets.

Having thus described my invention, what I claim as new, and desire to secure by Letters Patent, is—

As a new article of manufacture, a pair of pantaloons having the pocket-openings secured at each edge by means of rivets, substantially in the manner described and shown, whereby the seams at the points named are prevented from ripping, as set forth.

In witness whereof I hereunto set my hand and seal.

JACOB W. DAVIS. [L. S.]

Witnesses:
JAMES C. HAGERMAN,
W. BERGMAN.

The patent notice for the use of rivets in the manufacturing of Levi's pants, submitted by Jacob Davis and the Levi Strauss Company.

that fact was destined to change the clothing habits of the whole country.

Not that most Americans were cowboys or cowgirls. Far from it. By the early part of the twentieth century, more and more people were moving to the cities. Fewer and fewer knew one end of a horse from the other. But even as the country became citified, the cowboy was becoming the great American hero, featured in books, magazines, movies and finally on television. As he became a legend, so did the clothes he wore. To share in that legend—even if you lived in the East—all you had to do was slip on a pair of Levi's. So, by the middle of the century, Levi's were not only western work clothes. Children wore them. Students wore them. Movie stars wore them. Even presidents of the United States wore them.

One of the more interesting parts of the story of Levi's is the name itself. Many inventions have been named for their creators. Almost always, it is the last name that has been used: Henry *Ford*, Louis *Braille*, Rudolph *Diesel*, Jules *Leotard*, Clarence *Birdseye*, just to name a few.

But Levi Strauss gave us his first name. Think about it. If he had had a more common name, today we might all be wearing a pair of Bill's or Jim's or Sam's.

Frontier to Fashion

◀Cowboys were the second group of hard workers who chose Levi's.

In the early years of the twentieth ▶ century, kids began to wear Levi's.

◀In the 1960s, denims became accepted leisure-time garb for adults as well as children.

◀ The 1970s saw denims gaining favor in all kinds of situations from travel to business.

The Legend of Levi's

Levi's have become as American as apple pie, but a lot more useful. So useful, in fact, that legends began to circulate about the durability and value of the pants.

One of the gorier tales features several workmen who were moving a number of old graves from the site of a planned shopping center in Sacramento, California. In one grave dated 1871 they found "the remains of an old-timer dressed in Levi's, and although the coffin, etc, had not weathered the passing years, the Levi's were still in fair condition." There is still another burial story that tells of a man who wished to take part in the planning of his own funeral. He purchased a coffin and wrote a letter which he hoped would be followed in every detail. Here is what he said: "When I should happen to die sometime I want to wear the preshrunk Levi's blue jeans, Levi's denim shirt and Levi's denim jacket."

More cheerful was an incident recalled by an ex-railroader:

"The Arizona Lumber Company at Flagstaff operated a logging train which ran from its sawmill in Flagstaff into its lumbering camps some thirteen miles away. The engine burned wood, and I and another boy were employed as firemen to feed great stocks of wood into the firebox. One day our engine was pulling seven heavily-loaded cars piled mountain high with immense, long logs. About two miles out from camp, the coupling link which connected the tender with the train broke. No other links were available, and owing to the strain on the heavily-loaded cars, none could be safely disconnected. Our engineer—wearing copper-riveted 'Levi's' (pants), as did all the men in Arizona at that time—took off his 'Levi's', soused them in the water tank, twisted them into a rope, tied them into a link connecting the engine with the train and proceeded on the journey to Flagstaff about ten miles away, and by the way, negotiated several heavy grades. Of all mankind's millions of useful inventions, none surpasses the service of the 'Levi's.'"

Years later, in 1972, the Levi Strauss Company duplicated that feat—on the Roaring Camp & Big Trees Narrow Gauge Railroad—for an advertisement.

Then there were some happenings which the company chose not to reenact. A construction worker wrote about the time he was working on a 52-story bank building in Ft. Worth, Texas. A crane hook caught him by the pocket of his Levi's and swung him out from the structure, dangling him in mid-air hundreds of feet above the ground. The worker thought himself a goner, but the pocket of his pants didn't rip. After a few minutes, the man was rescued. He urged the Levi Strauss Company to ". . . keep putting Levi's out; you have the best. Levi's saved my life so I pass it (the word) around."

Of course there were occasional complaints. One customer grumbled:

The enclosed pair of pants are being returned because they didn't wear very well. According to your guarante (guarantee) maybe you will replace them. In the last few weeks the back seems (seams) came out and had to be resewed. Then the pockets tore loose and next the material in the leg just started falling apart. Even resewing doesn't help. We are quite disappointed as they were only bought in 1948—worn maybe twict (twice) a week and only washed once a month. We've never had this trouble before.

The letter was dated August 1965.

Levi's famous trademark suggests the legendary strength of a pair of denims.

Old tools used in the manufacture of Levi's jeans include a knife (bottom left) which was used to cut through 18 layers of heavy-weight denim; tongs for lifting the bolts of fabric; and a mallet and punch for attaching the well-known rivets.

The Levi Strauss History Room, located in the company's headquarters in downtown San Francisco, is the world's only blue jeans museum. It contains photographs, tools, letters and old pairs of pants that tell the story of Levi's from the beginning in 1850.

Exhibits include several pairs of pants returned to the Company by their owners for safekeeping. This pair served a man who wore them every day except Sunday for two years. He returned them in 1920 with a letter asking what went wrong: "I have worn nothing but Levi Strauss overalls for the last 30 years and this pair has not given me the service that I have gotten out of some of your overalls in the past."

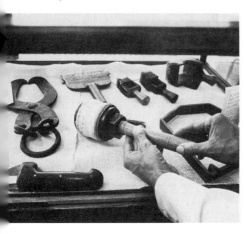

This old pair of jeans was used to tow a car out of the mud. A California man whose car was stuck found only the two short pieces of rope and a pair of old Levi's in the trunk. He remembered the famous two-horse brand which had by then been worn off the leather patch and decided he had nothing to lose by trying a modern version of this test of strength. The pants passed the test.

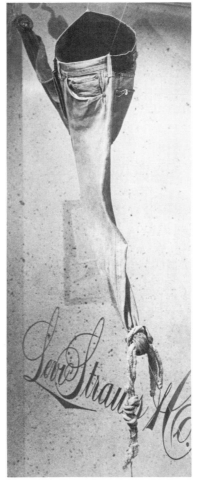

How Levi's Are Made

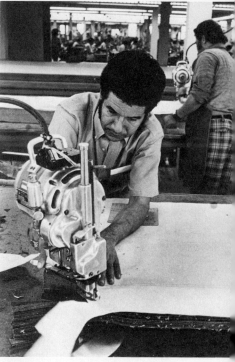

Behind the scenes at a Levi's plant. In the first step, denim is spread for cutting on 100-foot long tables by pushing a spreader back and forth on tracks which run the length of the table.

An electric cutter with a vertical knife edge is used to cut through 20 or more layers of denim. Paper patterns stapled to the top layer serve as a guideline.

In the sewing room, half-finished jeans are ready for side-seaming.

Levi's arcuate (V-shaped), trademark design is sewn on back pockets with a double-needle sewing machine in one continuous operation. Later, the connecting threads will be snipped, and the pockets stacked for the next operation—sewing them on the back of the jeans.

A sewing machine operator attaches belt loops to the waistband of a nearly completed pair of jeans. The V-shaped design—called an "arcuate"—on the back pocket is the world's oldest apparel trademark.

How to Dress Them Up

A gallery of winners in the Levi's Denim Art Contest.

How to Embroider Your Jeans ❀

Here are a few simple stitches you can use to decorate your Levi's. By combining stitches, varying their length and direction, and using different colors of embroidery thread, you can make all kinds of attractive designs.

The *running stitch* is the simplest embroidery stitch. Simply run the needle in and out of the cloth and pull. The result is a series of 'dashes'.

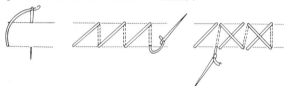

To make the *cross-stitch* draw two parallel guidelines. Bring the thread up from underneath on the lower line, then go back into the cloth a short distance to the right

on the upper line. Keep the needle at right angles to the guidelines and bring the thread out directly beneath the last entry point. Repeat this process to make a series of angled stitches. Then work back the other way, crossing each stitch. The final result will look like a series of X's.

Begin the *straight stitch* by bringing the thread up from underneath the cloth, then go back in a short distance away. Bring the thread up where you want the second stitch to begin and repeat the process. You can vary the distance between stitches and the lengths of the stitches themselves. You can also butt the ends of two stitches together or work stitches into circles or other patterns.

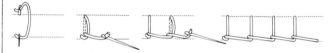

The *blanket stitch* looks like a row of interlocking L's. Once again make two guidelines. Bring the thread up on the bottom line, then back in on the top line a

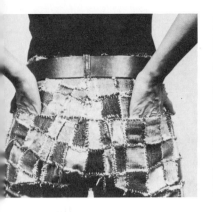

Levi's may start out as mass-produced garments, but they don't always end up that way. Many customers devote themselves to individualizing their denims. In fact, over the years they have created a new kind of folk art. Realizing this, in 1973 the Levi Strauss Company held a national denim decorating contest. The rules required only that the clothes be wearable, reasonably durable and creatively adorned.

The results were incredible. Some two thousand entries came from nearly every state in the union. The denims were painted, patched, embroidered, crocheted, appliqued, photo silk-screened, macramed, bedecked with rhinestones and even feathered. They featured rainbows, suns, moons, cartoon characters and landscape scenes.

The winning entry was a Levi's denim jacket decorated with eleven pounds of silver, brass and jewel-toned studs; a police whistle; a removable ashtray; a desk bell and assorted ribbon and button trims. Bill Shire, a Los Angeles craftsman, spent 200 hours remodeling his jacket.

The entries were so impressive that the top twenty-five were packaged as an art show that opened at the Museum of Contemporary Crafts in New York City and then toured the United States and Europe. Levi's had come a long, long way for a product originally designed to stand up to the dirt and stress of gold mines and cattle drives.

short distance to the right. Bring the needle back up through the material just to the right of where it first came out. Pass the needle over the thread and pull it snug to make the first L. Push the needle back in on the upper line, and bring it back out on the lower line, once again crossing over the thread. Repeat the stitch, pulling the thread up snuggly each time to make the L's.

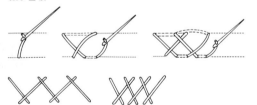

The finished *herringbone stitch* looks like an old-fashioned rail fence. Once more work between two guidelines. Bring the thread up through the material on the lower line. Go back in on the top line a short distance to the right. Then bring the thread out to the left of the starting point. Make an X by bringing the thread *under* the first leg of the stitch. Now make a second X, overlapping the first leg of the last stitch. Bring the thread *over* that leg and *under* the first leg of the new one. Repeat the process. You may vary the pattern by changing the angle of the legs of the X's. You may also change the distance between the guidelines or use curved lines.

Another way to decorate your jeans is with an *applique* (pronouned ap-la-kā). An applique is a piece of cloth cut to shape and stitched onto another piece of cloth. In this drawing, the star was cut from a brightly-colored rag and stitched to a pair of Levi's. The flowers were made by working blanket stitches in a circle, and the numbers were formed with cross-stitches.

There are many more stitches and styles in embroidery. If you'd like to learn about them, your library or bookstore will have several good books on the subject. One excellent introduction to embroidery and thread art of all kinds is *Painting With Stitches: A Guide to Embroidery, Needlepoint, Crochet & Macrame* by Vera P. Guild (Sterling, 1976).

How to Recycle Your Denims

Use it up,
Wear it out;
Make it do,
Or do without.
New England Maxim

Even the Levi Strauss Company admits that sooner or later denims will wear out. But that doesn't mean they have to be thrown away. The Company has collected a pocketful of suggestions for keeping their pants in use no matter how much abuse they've taken.

A cap

If you've ever wanted a hat with pockets (and who hasn't?), here's your chance. It's easy if you're handy with a sewing machine, or if you have a friend who's handy and owes you a favor.

Step 1. Make a paper pattern shaped like an elongated oval 3½ inches wide by about 10 inches long. Trace the pattern eight times on pieces of cut-apart jeans. Include two pocket pieces, a rivet, a tab or other interesting parts of the old pants.

Step 2. Cut out the pieces and sew them together to form the shell of the cap. Sew together two crescent-shaped pieces along the outer edge to make a visor and slip a piece of cardboard or plastic of the same shape inside for stiffness.

Step 3. For the lining, sew a strip of satin— 4 inches wide and approximately 2 inches longer than your head measures around—to a 10-inch circle of the same satin material and fit it inside the denim shell.

Step 4. Pin the shell, lining and visor together. Place a strip of imitation-leather binding, about 1¼ inches wide, to the right side of the denim along the edge to act as a sweatband. Sew the four pieces together, then turn the sweatband in. Top the cap with a button from the jeans.

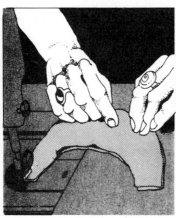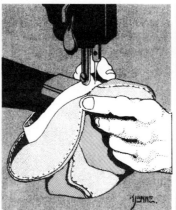

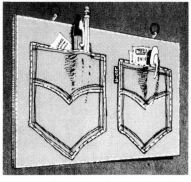

A pencil and letter holder

Cut a rectangular piece from the back of a pair of jeans leaving the back pockets in place. Tack the piece onto a varnished board. Hang it over your desk or next to the telephone.

Pants for a plant

To dress up a plant pot, simply cut off a section from the leg portion of some discarded denims and slip it over the pot. If necessary, stitch a seam along the length to make it fit snugly. For decoration, you can sew on some pockets.

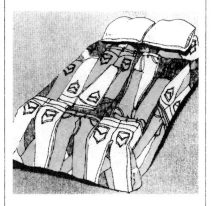

A bedspread

Cut apart and sew together material from lots of old blue jeans. Then, some morning when you're feeling lazy and you hear the call to get up, you can stay in bed and still honestly announce, "I've already got my pants on."

A purse

It's not easy, according to the old saying, to make a silk purse out of a pig's ear. But, you can make an attractive carrying bag out of an old pair of pants.

Step 1. Cut off the legs from a pair of jeans.

Step 2. Sew the bottom of the leg holes closed.

Step 3. Cut a narrow strip from one of the legs for use as a shoulder strap.

Step 4. Decorate the purse with embroidery, metal studs or whatever suits your fancy.

How to be a Rodeo Star

The life of a rodeo rider isn't easy. Unlike most professional sports stars, rodeo people do not belong to teams or have managers and promoters. Each rider follows the circuit from rodeo to rodeo, living on what prize money he can earn. Sometimes the rodeo is a family affair, with husband, wife and older children all competing in different events.

One of the top events in the rodeo is *saddle bronc riding*. The object is to ride a bucking horse for ten seconds. That's not quite as easy as it sounds. A bronc can't stand anything on his back, and he won't stop kicking until he has thrown you off.

You mount your bronc in a chute which connects with the main ring. A rope rein has been attached to the horse's halter. You take the rein in one hand and must leave the other hand free throughout the ride. If you switch hands on the rein or touch the horse with your free hand, you'll be disqualified. A gate opens, letting the horse into the ring. Usually he'll come out of the chute already in the air, landing on his front feet and kicking his hind legs, then jerking from one side to the other, trying to toss you off.

Just holding tight for ten seconds isn't enough to win first place. A judge will be awarding you up to 25 points for style. You'll be expected to 'lick' the horse—that means you'll be rocking forward and back, lifting your heels to spur the horse high in front, then swinging your legs back to spur him high behind. A good rhythmic lick will bring you valuable points.

The bronc has his own judge. While your style is being checked out, the horse judge is scoring how tough your mount is. The wilder the ride, the higher the score. Top score is again 25. Your bronc is chosen by lot before the event, and you don't get a chance to test him out first. All cowboys hope for the roughest ride they can get, for if the horse fizzles out or bucks in a predictable pattern, he'll

Calf roping. The clock starts and your horse thunders into the ring. You hold your lariat ready to toss the moment the calf comes within range.

A smooth, accurate toss settles the loop over the calf's head. You tie the rope to the saddle horn as your horse digs in.

pull a low score and kill your chances to win first place.

Bull riding is similar to bronc riding, but this time your mount is a Brahman bull which can weigh up to a ton. If you thought bronc riding was the most dangerous sport, you'll change your mind after you try one of these foul-tempered monsters. Broncs, after they throw you, usually calm down and leave you alone to pick yourself up out of the mud. Bulls, on the other hand, aren't satisfied until they have wiped the ring with you.

For this reason, two rodeo clowns share the ring with you. These two daredevils are there to distract the bull and pull you to safety should you take a fall. One clown has a barrel which he uses both as a noisemaker to attract the bull and a shelter to hide in if the bull charges.

You ride a bull barebacked. Your only handhold is a rope tied loosely around the animal's middle. You twist the rope around your hand and hang on for dear life. Though the rope helps you hang on, it might also kill you. Sometimes a rider will be thrown, but snag his foot in the rope on the way to the

The horse holds tension on the rope while you wrestle the calf to the ground and collect three feet.

Done! The feet are tied and the clock stops.

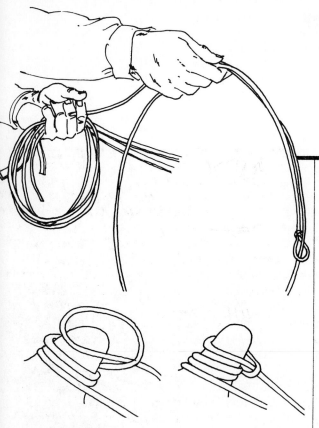

Holding the lariat. The loop of the lariat is held in the throwing hand, with the eyelet, or honda, about quarter way down the loop. The thumb and forefinger of the other hand play out rope while the other fingers handle the reins.

Tying off the rope. When the calf is lassoed, the rider takes a couple of turns around the saddle horn, securing the rope with a half-hitch. The half-hitch is made by forming a loop in the main line of the rope, flipping it over so the main line is beneath the loop, and dropping the loop over the saddle horn. The harder the rope is tugged, the tighter the knot will hold. With practice, you can make a half-hitch with one hand in a second or less.

What's more, the drama of the event also makes it the most popular with the crowds.

Calf roping is an event which demands the very best from a cowboy and his horse. The object is to chase a calf into the ring, lasso it, throw it to the ground and tie together three of its feet, all in the shortest possible time. Teamwork between rider and horse is a must.

You and your horse wait behind a barrier for the calf to be released. In one hand you hold the loop of your lariat. In the other are the coils of the lariat and your reins. Between your teeth you hold a shorter length of rope which you'll use to tie the calf.

The calf is let into the arena. You start your horse moving toward the barrier, which will be opened by a piece of cord attached to the calf's neck. You want to time it just right so that you pass through the opening at top speed just as the barrier opens. You must be precise, because if you hit the barrier too soon, a penalty of ten seconds is added to your score. The penalty can mean disaster, as competitors sometimes win by mere fractions of a second.

Once you've caught up with the calf, you lasso it round the neck. Your horse will immediately dig in, yanking the calf to a halt. You quickly tie the rope to your saddle and dismount. Chances are the roping has already pulled the calf off its feet. If so, you must allow it to get back up and then throw it to the ground yourself. Meanwhile your horse is keeping the lasso taut so the calf won't be able to run off again. You capture three of the kicking feet and tie them off. The clock is stopped and your time recorded.

ground. If this happens, you'll find yourself being dragged beside or under four thrashing hooves. The barrel clown will pound his barrel to get the bull's attention while his partner takes his own life into his hands by getting close enough to cut you free.

Bull riding is the most deadly of all the rodeo events, but it also brings the best money.

How a Zipper Works

The first Levi's pants did not have zippers for the simple reason that the zipper had not yet been invented.

It wasn't until 1893 that Whitcomb L. Judson devised a way to fasten together two thin metal chains by pulling a slider between them. He founded the Automatic Hook and Eye Company in Meadville, Pennsylvania, intending at first to sell his product to boot and shoe manufacturers. Judson thought his "Universal Fastener" would make it much easier to put on or take off footwear. Judson's partner, Lewis Walker, was more ambitious. He dreamed of the day when their device would replace buttons and hooks on all kinds of clothing.

The masses, however, weren't very interested in either use of the product. For nearly two decades, Judson and Walker struggled on with little success. Then they were joined by another inventor, Gideon Sunback, who had come up with some important improvements in the basic Judson model. The big break came when the United States Army ordered a great quantity of fasteners for use on military uniforms.

Many years later, someone at the B. F. Goodrich Company came up with the name "Zipper," presumably because of the "zipping" sound the device makes. The name was registered, but it became so popular, people used it for all kinds of hookless fasteners, not just those made by the Goodrich Company. Thus, the word, like other once-trademarked names such as aspirin, cellophane, escalator, linoleum and mimeograph, became an "ordinary" English word, spelled with a lower case "z" and free to be used by anyone.

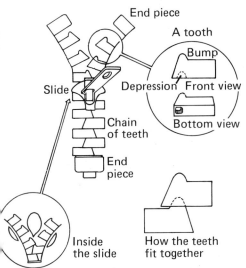

End piece
A tooth
Bump
Depression Front view
Bottom view
Slide
Chain of teeth
End piece
Inside the slide
How the teeth fit together

A zipper holds two pieces of cloth together by interlocking two chains of tiny metal teeth. Each tooth has a bump on the top and a depression on the bottom the same shape as the bump. The two rows of teeth are staggered, so that when the two halves of the zipper are brought together, the bump in one tooth fits into the depression of the one above it, locking them together.

The teeth are pressed together by the slider. Inside the slider is a separator like a traffic island which forms a Y-shaped channel. One row of teeth runs through each arm of the Y. When the zipper is pulled up, the channel forces the teeth between each other and the zipper closes.

End pieces keep the slider from falling off the zipper. The end piece on the bottom of the zipper on a jacket also holds the ends of the zipper together by sliding a piece of metal into a slot. This keeps the bottom of the zipper from being pulled apart.

McDonald's

Richard J. McDonald (left) and Maurice J. McDonald (right), cofounders of McDonald's.

Once upon a time there lived two brothers named McDonald; they didn't have a farm. Instead, they owned a hamburger stand in San Bernardino, California. They didn't know it, but their place was going to change the eating habits of people around the world.

Richard and Maurice ("Mac") McDonald had moved from New Hampshire to Southern California during the 1920s. Like a lot of young people, they were attracted to the glamour of Hollywood and the movies. They didn't become movie stars, but instead spent several years back stage moving scenery, handling the lights, driving the trucks with equipment and doing other odd jobs. In 1932, they bought a run-down movie theater and began to show movies. Their favorite part of that business must have been serving popcorn and other snacks because several years later they sold the theater and opened up a drive-in restaurant. Customers could be served right in their cars. Or they could eat in the restaurant.

Business was only so-so. For several years, the brothers tried to figure out a new approach to serving food. After discarding many schemes, they came up with a plan for an entirely new kind of restaurant. It would be self-service. People would line up at a window to pick up their orders. There would be no tables to wait on. The menu would list only a few items. Food would be served in paper containers leaving no plates or silverware to wash.

"When we told a few of our friends what we had in mind," recalled Richard McDonald years later, "they thought we had gone insane. They said they wouldn't patronize us if they had to serve themselves and if all we were going to sell were hamburgers, fries and drinks." But the two brothers decided to give it a try anyway.

At first it looked as if their friends had been right. On opening day only a few customers drove up, and these stayed in their cars, honking for service. The few customers who did

The original McDonald brothers' self-service hamburger stand. It opened in 1949 in San Bernardino, California. The Golden Arches weren't added until several years later.

come in were not satisfied. With the old-style restaurant, they could have their hamburgers prepared any way they liked, with mayonnaise, lettuce, tomato, barbecue sauce or whatever. But with the new system, the hamburger was prepared only one way. The customer had no choice. Some people got angry. One person shouted, "If the McDonald brothers are so cheap that they can't buy a jar of mayonnaise, I'll donate some to the store."

Things got so bad that the employees were ordered to park their own cars out front to make it look as if the stand were doing a little business.

For months, it seemed as though the new idea was going to be a bust. The old customers would not accept the changes. But then gradually, new people started coming in. Sales clerks, mechanics and other workers heard that they could get their orders filled in a couple of minutes and have the rest of their lunch hour free to do whatever they wanted to. They liked the price—only 15¢ for a hamburger and 10¢ for the fries. (Then, as now, the biggest profit came from the fries, which were much cheaper to make than the burgers.)

Before a year went by, business began to snowball. Now the McDonald brothers had a new problem. The lines of customers were so long, the system was bogging down. Sometimes there would be too many hamburgers but not enough fries. Or too many fries and not enough milkshakes.

It was at this point that Richard and Mac began to look at their business as a kind of science. They started designing new equipment, rearranging the kitchen, trying anything that might speed up the system. They developed a dispenser that would put mustard and catsup on six buns a second. They asked General Electric to produce a giant stainless steel griddle that was 6 feet long and 1 inch thick. They ordered a machine that could make six milkshakes at a time.

Gradually, the system improved. And as it did, word of the place spread throughout the Los Angeles area. No longer was McDonald's just a restaurant for workers. Families began to come on the weekends. Eating there was like going on a picnic, except that there was concrete underfoot rather than grass. Kids loved it. So did their parents, who didn't have to cook.

To make sure no one would miss the stand while driving by, the brothers hired a sign maker to create two giant neon arches. The glowing arches drew people in from near and far. Business boomed.

The McDonalds might have lived happily forever after, grilling burgers. They had all the success they wanted. But the same wasn't true for a man named Ray Kroc who paid them a visit one day in 1954.

One of Ray Kroc's goals in life was to strike it rich. He wanted money to flow the way water does when you turn on a faucet.

Born in 1902, he grew up in Chicago during a time when 20,000 Americans were becoming millionaires. He wanted to be one of them and believed it was possible if he worked hard enough. Persistence, he felt, was the key to success.

When Ray Kroc was four years old, his father took him to a phrenologist, a fortune-teller who tries to predict a person's future by studying the shape and bumps of the head. The phrenologist claimed that little Ray would find riches in either music or food.

Kroc tried music first. After serving as an ambulance driver in France during World War I (a young kid named Walt Disney was in the same company), he played piano in a number of bands in Chicago and in Florida.

When music didn't pay off, Kroc began a career as a salesman. He first sold Lily-Tulip paper cups, then real estate in Florida, and then finally became the sole distributor for a device called the Prince Castle Multimixer, a gadget that could make six milkshakes at the same time. Kroc went around the country selling the Multimixer. He got a chance to visit all kinds of restaurants and fast-food places. He was learning a lot but he wasn't sure what for. Still he pushed on.

In 1954, Ray Kroc was 52 years old. Many people at that age are thinking about retirement. But retiring was the last thing on Ray Kroc's mind. He still believed opportunity would knock. The "knock" came in the form of an order for eight of his Multimixers for a single restaurant. Kroc wanted to see for himself what kind of place needed to make forty-eight milkshakes at one time. So like a lot of other fortune seekers before him, he headed for California.

When Kroc got a glimpse of the McDonald brothers' hamburger stand, it was love at first sight. For a day he watched crowds of hungry people come and crowds of satisfied people go. He studied the efficient way the hamburgers were turned out. He inspected the immaculately clean restrooms. (He already knew, from his travels with the Multimixer, that a clean restroom meant a lot to most American families.)

To the mobs of people hurrying up to the stand, McDonald's was just a place to get fed, fast and cheap. To Ray Kroc, McDonald's was a beautifully designed machine for grinding out burgers the way a Ford plant cranked out cars. It was an incredible money-making machine with a cozy name—"McDonald's." Thanks to the old nursery rhyme, people everywhere were already familiar with the name and felt good about it.

After studying the operation for a day, Kroc told the McDonald brothers that he wanted to help them make McDonald's into a national chain. He would sell people licenses to open up their own McDonald's stands. The brothers would get some of the money each store earned. So would Kroc.

At first the McDonalds weren't interested. They had already sold a few licenses themselves. But Kroc, if anything, was persistent. After a few days he convinced them to let him try it. For the next six years, Kroc went around the country selling McDonald's licenses. It was hard work at first. Few people realized what a McDonald's stand could be worth.

The Multimixer milkshake machine that led Ray Kroc to the McDonald brothers.

Ray Kroc, the man who took the McDonald brothers' idea and turned it into a worldwide business.

(Today some of them bring in over a million dollars a year.)

Gradually, Kroc's stick-to-itiveness began to pay off. And all kinds of people gave up their jobs and went into the burger business. They came from all walks of life: policemen, realtors, teachers, doctors and other professionals. One lawyer explained why he gave up his law books for burgers: "I was so fascinated with it that I began spending more time at McDonald's than with my law practice. Finally, my law partner suggested that I spend full time at one place or the other. I chose McDonald's."

The McDonald brothers were happy. Money was flowing in. But Ray Kroc was not making the fortune he wanted. The trouble, he felt, was that the brothers had too much control.

For instance, they still made all the decisions about how each store would look and be operated. Kroc wanted to run the show his way.

Finally, in 1960, he decided to buy the brothers out. They were not really interested in selling, but to get the man off their backs, they told him he could have the whole thing for $2.7 million. Kroc was sitting in his office in a Chicago skyscraper when he heard the price. He dropped the phone. Dick McDonald, who was on the other end of the line, asked what the noise was. Kroc replied, "Just me jumping from the twentieth floor of the LaSalle-Wacker Building."

But Kroc didn't jump. Instead he surprised the McDonald brothers by agreeing to their price. The only hitch was that he did not have

$2.7 million or anything near it. With the help of a friend he was able to borrow the money—at a tremendously high rate of interest. "The $2.7 million ended up costing me $14 million," he said later. "But I guess there was no other way out. I needed the McDonald name and those golden arches. What are you going to do with a name like Kroc?"

Now that he owned McDonald's, one of Ray Kroc's first goals was to complete the job that the McDonald brothers had started: converting the ancient art of cooking into a modern science. So, instead of hiring chefs for his restaurants, Kroc hired engineers. He told them to create a space-age food-preparation system that would depend on machines, not people. He wanted a hamburger served in Portland, Maine, to taste exactly like one served in San Diego, California.

The engineers came through. They designed computer-controlled machines that would stamp out identical patties, each one weighing exactly 1.6 ounces, each one measuring 3.875 inches in diameter. They invented transistorized grills that told the burger-turner exactly when to flip over the burgers. They created a special French fries scooper that precisely controlled the number of fries to be stuffed into a bag.

In addition to creating foolproof machines that guaranteed uniform portions and cooking times, the McDonald's planners laid down guidelines for the human workers.

Once grilled, burgers could be kept warming under infrared lights for only 10 minutes; then they had to be thrown away. French fries were tossed out after 7 minutes. Coffee had to be served within 30 minutes of brewing. Windows had to be washed once a day. The parking lot had to be swept each hour.

The system did not get rid of people altogether, but it obviously did not require highly skilled workers. If it had, their high salaries would have made it impossible for McDonald's to sell food so cheaply.

What Kroc needed were smiling faces and willing hands. He found them among the high-school-age kids of the country. Some people who do not like McDonald's complain that the system takes advantage of young people. They say that it gives them mainly boring jobs to do at low pay. And, in fact, many of the young workers quit their jobs after only a few weeks or a few months.

But other people point out that there isn't very much work for young people in this country and that McDonald's has created thousands of jobs where there were few before. Many of the McDonald's workers say they enjoy their time at McDonald's because they like meeting people. Others feel they learn a great deal about running a business. Finally, there is a chance for advancement. The current president of the company started out grilling hamburgers in Ray Kroc's first franchise. Fifteen years later, he was running the billion dollar business.

While the engineers were inventing new ways to computerize the burger, Kroc's advertising writers were dreaming up new ways to sell it. Knowing that most people like a winner, they spent a lot of time telling how successful the chain was. In 1973, when over 12 billion burgers had been sold, the company announced that if all those hamburgers were stacked in one pile. They would form a mountain 783

When McDonald's first began, most people in Japan didn't even know what a hamburger was. Now they eat millions of them a year. In fact, the busiest McDonald's unit in the world is in Tokyo.

Ronald McDonald in a TV commercial.

times bigger than the biggest pyramid in Egypt. Later they pointed out that if someone could eat a burger every five minutes, it would take 114,000 years to consume those 12 billion burgers. On the other hand, if all the cattle that had been ground up to make those patties were alive and well, they would cover an area larger than London, England. (How the Londoners would feel about that, no one said.)

When the advertising people got tired of talking numbers, they created a clown named Ronald McDonald. (At one point there were fifty full-time Ronalds.) The clown not only appeared in television ads but also for fund-raising activities around the country. Ray Kroc insisted that each McDonald's support home-town charities and pitch in during floods or other emergencies. It was important to make McDonald's a real part of the community.

Finally, there were the songs and the jingles. "You deserve a break today" and "We do it all for you" became almost as familiar as "The Star Spangled Banner." The aim was to create the idea that people go to McDonald's, not just because they're hungry but because it's a neat thing to do.

Kroc summed up his whole approach in a formula known by the letters "QSC/TLC" which translated into the phrase "Quality Service Cleanliness/Tender Loving Care." For those who might find the formula too hard to grasp, the Hamburger King boiled it down even further, into a motto he borrowed from Colonel Sanders: KISS—"Keep It Simple, Stupid."

The system worked. By 1972, Kroc had made the fortune that he had long dreamed of. He was worth half a billion dollars and was one of the twenty richest people in the United States. He was 70 years old, long past the age of retirement. And so . . . he bought the San Diego Padres baseball team and began a new career as a sportsman.

From Beef to Burger

Not so long ago, people knew exactly where the meat they ate came from. They hunted game. They raised and slaughtered livestock. They caught their own fish. Nowadays, most of us buy meat at the supermarket or ready to eat at a restaurant. But it may still be worth knowing where it comes from and how it gets to us.

Most beef cattle in the United States start their lives on the ranches of the West or the Southwest. Some 500 million acres of farmland are in grass. An additional 400 million acres are in uncultivated range land.

After a summer of grazing, or sometimes at the end of the second summer, the calves are sold to livestock producers called "feeders." Feeders put the young cattle on a special diet of grain and other feeds to fatten and finish them for the market. Seventy-five percent of all feed consumed by cattle is grass, forage and by-products which are inedible by humans. For example,

cottonseed and soybeans are fed to livestock after the oil has been pressed out of them. The pulp and tops of sugar beets and the pulp of citrus fruit are used as feed. Animals are also fed dehydrated meat and bone scraps left over from the meat-packing operations.

One quarter of cattle feed is grain—mainly corn—that could be consumed by humans. Cattle do not have to be finished on a grain diet to produce nutritious meat. Grain and other concentrated food

are used because they help cattle put on weight faster and make meat more flavorful.

Some critics of the high-meat diet eaten by most Americans say that if people here ate less meat, there would be a lot more grain available to deal with the worldwide hunger problem. As of now, Americans on the average eat about 175 pounds of meat a year, double the amount eaten ten years ago.

When animals are ready for slaughter, they are sent to public markets. Animals may be slaughtered on the same day they are purchased by a packer, or they may be held for a few days in the yards, depending on the schedule of the slaughtering plant.

In the slaughterhouse, the first step is to knock the cattle unconscious with a cartridge-powered or air-powered hammer called a "stunner."

The animal is then elevated with the head down and killed by someone called a "sticker" who cuts the main blood vessels in the neck. Rapid and complete bleeding is necessary to protect the quality of the meat.

As soon as the blood has drained, the animals are skinned. An inspector checks the internal organs to make sure that the animal was free of disease.

The carcass is now split into halves, trimmed, washed, shrouded (covered with heavy cotton fabric), and moved into chilling rooms where the temperature stays just above the freezing point.

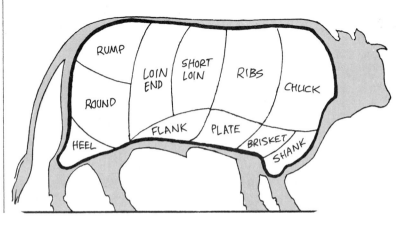

This is the production line of Keystone Foods Corporation, the company which provides nearly half the hamburger patties for McDonald's. After being graded and inspected, the beef is ground up and put in big wheeled hoppers. Workers push the hoppers to the starting end of the assembly line. After that, the machines take over.

The hamburger machine turns the ground meat into millions of patties, all precisely the same size, shape and weight.

The operation is controlled by computer from this control room.

Keystone Foods also provides McDonald's with other supplies, like forks, napkins, salt, catsup and coffee. These are kept in a huge warehouse. When the time comes to make a shipment to the restaurants, the supplies and the frozen burgers are loaded onto trucks...

...and unloaded at the restaurants. The frozen hamburger is popped into the store's freezer to be ready for the next day's crowds.

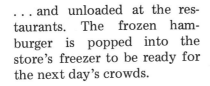

Behind the Scenes at a McDonald's

While standing in line at a McDonald's, do you ever wonder what's going on back in the kitchen? If so, here's your chance to find out.

Frozen meat patties, stacked in a bin next to the grill, wait to be turned into Big Macs and other goodies.

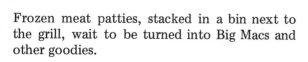

When the call comes to make some burgers, the first step is to put the buns into the toaster.

Next, the patties are slapped onto the grill. Note the electronic timer to the right of the worker's head that signals when each stage of the cooking is done.

The grill person presses each patty with a spatula in order to sear it and seal in the juices.

Another crew member uses a stainless steel dispenser that squirts exactly the right amount of catsup onto the toasted buns. The containers lined up on the table hold lettuce, pickles, onions and cheese used to "dress" the buns.

Another worker loads apple pies fresh from the fryer into their individual packages.

Meanwhile, the French fries stand ready, kept hot by infrared lamps. The scooper in the foreground measures a precise number of fries into each bag.

Back at the grill, finished meat patties are placed on the dressed buns.

The completed burgers are carried on trays up front where they are wrapped or placed in boxes.

Cokes flow from an automatic machine that premeasures each serving.

At regular intervals, during all this food-making activity, crew members take time to keep the place clean.

Working at McDonald's

To find out what it's like to work at McDonald's, we interviewed a seventeen-year-old female employee. Obviously, she cannot speak for the nearly one million other McDonald's workers, but she does talk openly about her own experiences. Her words should give you some idea about what happens when you have a job at the Golden Arches.

Q: How did you get your job at McDonald's?
A: It was posted on a bulletin board at the local shopping center. I went to a McDonald's and filled out an application. A few days later they interviewed me. The next day the guy called me up and said I had the job.

Q: Did the interviewer ask you a lot of questions?
A: Not really. We just sat down in the store. He read over my application.

Q: That was all there was to your interview?
A: Yes. It was pretty simple. I was scared. I expected it to be something different.

Q: How old were you then?
A: I was 16. You can be 15½ when you apply but you can't start working until you're 16.

Q: What kind of training did you get?
A: We went to two orientation meetings. We saw filmstrips that explained how to do various jobs there. One was called "The Six Window Steps," and it explains how to wait on people. During these meetings, they also took us on a tour through the place. And then we had a test run where we actually worked the grills, and we worked window. Some of us would pretend we were customers and order things while the other trainees filled the orders. Then we'd switch roles.

Q: Did they teach you how to grill hamburgers?
A: I didn't learn how to grill until a couple of months after I'd been working window.

Q: You mentioned the six window steps. What are they?
A: First, greet the customer and take their order. Second, suggest something else; like if they order a small Coke, fries and a hamburger, you ask them if they want a hot apple pie or a sundae. Third, you tell them how much the order costs. Fourth, you go assemble it. Fifth, you take their money. And sixth, you say, "Thank you. Come back soon."

Q: All that's explained in the filmstrip?
A: Yes. It shows a crew person who's completely neat, her hair is up, and she's bright and cheery and smiling.

We also have a videotape machine in our crew room, and it has tapes for everything. If you want to study how to do grill, you just ask the manager for the key. It's really helpful. Even if you already know how to do something, it's kind of interesting to refresh your memory from time to time.

Q: Is there just one right way to do each job?
A: Well, the managers are always saying that I'm changing everything. But then they always add "for the better." I take some rules and turn them around to find a better way of doing something. I'm talking mostly about simple things. I'll be doing something the way they trained me for a while and then I'll just switch

to a way that's faster and easier for me. Then a manager will come up and start doing it the official way. But after I show him my way, he'll usually say, "Yeah, that's a good way."

Q: Don't they criticize you for doing it your own way?
A: No, not unless it slows down the work. I even described one of my tricks in the crew newspaper. I explained a better way to arrange the utensil dish for breakfast.

Q: You mentioned the "crew room." What's that?
A: It's the workers' place. We have a dressing room with lockers and a space with a table and chairs where we can relax. Our crew has fixed it up just the way we like it. We pitched in two bucks each and bought a stereo set.

Q: Sounds like there's real team spirit.
A: Yes. There's lots of it at our store. Most of our workers have been at the place for nearly a year. When new people come, we always make sure they feel at home immediately. And we have lots of parties. We're one big group. We stick together.

Q: How many people work at your store?
A: About seventy.

Q: Are there any older people?
A: A woman I just trained has kids in high school. She really likes having this extra job. She says she's so busy, she's losing weight.

Q: I wonder if you can give some details about your work. For instance, what's it like to work grill?
A: Well, grill is really confusing at first. I still don't work it very often. But the main thing is I know how to work it whenever they need me.

Q: Exactly how is it done?
A: O.K. Say you get an order for 12 hamburgers. The first thing you do is put the top of the buns face up on a metal tray and put them into the toaster. You pull the handle down, sort of like a waffle iron, to start them toasting. A buzzer will go off when they're ready.

Then you take the hamburger patties out of the bin and line them up on the grill, 6 in a row. You press each one down to sear it. That keeps the juices in. Then a buzzer on the grill will tell you when to turn the patties over to cook them on the other side. It only takes a couple of minutes to do them.

While the burgers are cooking, the toaster buzzer will sound. You take out your top buns and then you put in the heels—that's the bottom part of the bun—right after that. As soon as you take out the top buns, you dress them. You put on a squirt of mustard and a squirt of catsup. The squirters put on just the right amount. And then you put on the pickles. Next you call "cheese order" to find out from whoever is managing the front how many of the burgers will have cheese on them. For example, if you're grilling twelve burgers, you'll call out, "Cheese on twelve burgers" and they'll call back, "Cheese four," so you put cheese on four of them, and the others will be plain.

Q: Does one person do everything?
A: If it's not busy, yes. But when it's super busy, you've got one person running meat, one person running buns, one person dressing the burgers (putting on the lettuce, the catsup, etc.), and one person wrapping them and putting them in the front bin ready to go.

Q: How does the person working grill know how many hamburgers to put on?
A: The person working bin up front keeps track of what's needed and calls the orders back to the grill.

Q: Is it true that food will be thrown away after a certain number of minutes?
A: Yes. Everything is done on ten-minute time restrictions. We put little numbers above each food slot that tell how long the food can stay there. And the managers are very strict about it because we get blitzed all the time. Blitzed is when inspectors or supervisors come into the store on surprise visits and grade us on everything.

Q: When the inspectors come in, do you talk to them?

A: Often I don't even know who they are. They don't send the same supervisor around too many times because you'd get to recognize them. So you never know. The first time I got blitzed, I was just in a carefree mood. This guy ordered a Coke. I said, "O.K.," and I went and got his Coke and said, "That'll be 30¢. I took his money and said, "O.K., thanks. Have a nice evening." He walked off, and I lost points for not suggesting that he get something else and for not saying "Thank you. Come back again." But he gave me an extra point because I was super friendly.

Q: Who gets all the things ready in the kitchen?

A: The breakfast grill does that. Right now I'm working from six A.M. to one-thirty so I sometimes open grill; that means, get everything set up. After I line up the eggs and other things I'll need for breakfast, I get the things ready for lunch. I take out the lettuce and put it in all the containers. I put the pickles in their containers. I get the cheese ready. I take the hamburger patties out of the freezer and put them into the refrigerator.

Q: Do you like working grill?

A: Yes, especially at breakfast because it's not so rushed.

Q: Are all the eggs pre-cracked?

A: No. I had one lady who saw our cook cracking eggs and she says, "Oh, I thought you used imitation eggs." But we don't. We use real eggs. We crack them as we get the orders. If someone wants an Egg McMuffin, we make it from scratch. We have these little rings that you crack the eggs into on the grill. The rings keep the fried eggs nice and round.

Q: Which do you prefer? Working grill or working window?

A: Probably window because I like working with the people. I like talking and smiling and making sure everything's good for the customers. In fact, in the morning, when we're not rushed, I take the food to the customers.

I get to know almost all the regulars. And they like my spirit.

Q: What are the customers like?

A: Most of them are fine. I get a few grouches. It depends on my mood, too. If I'm in a bad mood that day, it's kind of hard. But I just have to cover up my mood and do my best.

But if I'm in a good mood and I get a grouch, I can usually get him out of it just by smiling. I'll be super-perky and say, "Thank you very much. Have a nice day." Then they'll smile and say, "Thank you, too."

Q: You mentioned outside inspectors. Do the managers in your store also check up on the way you do your job?

A: Yes. Everyday as a matter of fact. We have a chart up on the wall, right by the time clock where you punch in your hours. The chart lists everyone's name and there's a space for every day of the month. They grade you everyday on the quality of your work. Green means poor work. Red means average. Blue means outstanding. The manager will watch you at work and then stick on a dot of one of the colors.

Q: Does the manager explain your rating for the day?

A: Yes, especially if you get a green. Actually, they can't even give you a green if first they give you a warning and if you correct the problem during your shift. If you correct it, they have to give you a red for the day.

Q: What kind of thing might lead to getting a poor rating?

A: Well, some of the things aren't really connected with the work itself. Like the other day, they gave someone a green for drinking milk. We get free food but we can't drink dairy products.

As for work, you'll get a green if you don't do all six window steps. They're not picky about it everyday. But if your manner is bad towards the public, or if you're always forgetting to say "Thank you, come back," or if you don't usually suggest something, they're going to get on you.

Q: Is your work on the grill also rated?
A: Yes. If you can't keep up with your orders, they'll get down on that. Or if you're making bad hamburgers.

Q: What's a bad hamburger?
A: If it's not seared properly, then it won't be juicy. Or sometimes if it is smashed, the person on grill will try to cover it up with onions.

Q: What about your appearance?
A: If they saw something they didn't like, for instance, if your hair was in your face, they'd bring that up.

Q: Do you ever have to do clean-up work?
A: Oh, yes. If I'm working window and there's a quiet time with no customers, I'll run out and check the lobby and clean it up.

Q: What's the lobby?
A: That's the area where the customers are.

Q: Are there times when your main job is cleaning up?
A: Right. Just the other day they put me on lobby for two hours. I didn't mind.

Q: You seem to enjoy working at McDonald's. Do you like the food?
A: Yes.

Q: Do you get tired of it?
A: Well, actually, we invent things that we can't sell to the public. Like we've fixed up omelettes and crepes. Plus we're allowed to make a BIG, BIG MAC, loaded with everything.

Q: Do you ever go into a McDonald's when you're not working there?
A: I do sometimes, not very often.

Q: What about advancement?
A: When I first got the job, I was thinking of keeping it for a year. But now I've been thinking seriously about staying with it through junior college and maybe becoming a swing manager. After that, I would like to go on to whatever work I'm going to do after college.

Q: What's a swing manager?
A: It's just below assistant manager. You don't have to wear a crew uniform. You do a lot of paper work and generally manage what's going on. You also order the food from the suppliers.

Q: Do your bosses encourage you to stay with the company?
A: They encourage me by showing me how to do things and always asking me if I want to know more.

Q: Have you ever known any women managers?
A: Yes. One of our swing managers is a woman.

Q: How do your friends feel about your working at McDonald's?
A: Well, half of my friends work with me at McDonald's. That's where I met them. My friends at school think it's fine. My very best friend works at Taco La Paz, and so I go there with her and she goes to McDonald's with me.

Q: Is there anything you dislike about working at McDonald's?
A: There are times when I complain. Sometimes the managers will get on my back when I don't feel they should and they haven't got a reason. That gets me aggravated. But mostly I get along fine with everyone.

Q: How much do you make a week?
A: It comes to around $80 or $90.

Q: Would you recommend the job to other people?
A: It depends on the person. If someone doesn't like McDonald's, I'd say no.

Q: Do you think this has been a good work experience for you?
A: Yes. The main thing I've learned is to have a lot of patience with the public, just being able to always look cheerful. You've always got to give way to the customer. Whatever the customer says, goes. That and just staying with the job takes a lot of stamina.

Hamburger History

John Montagu, the Earl of Sandwich.

The hamburger has nothing at all to do with ham. It gets its name from the town of Hamburg, Germany. But if you want the whole story, you have to go back to ancient Rome.

According to food historians, the Romans thought up the idea of eating meat and other foods between pieces of bread. They called their invention an *offula*.

We might be using that same word today—imagine, a peanut butter and jelly offula—except for an Englishman named John Montagu, who lived from 1718 until 1792. Montagu was a nobleman whose official title was the Earl of Sandwich.

Around the time the American colonies were starting their revolution against England, Montagu was in charge of the British Navy. He was more famous, however, for playing cards and gambling. According to some historians, he enjoyed cards so much, he didn't want to interrupt the game by using a knife and fork to eat. Instead he placed the meat between two slices of bread so he could pick it up with one hand. We should note that fans of Montagu say the Earl really started eating this way because he was so busy running the navy.

Which story is true, no one knows. Nor can historians tell us whether or not Montagu knew about the Roman *offula*. But his way of eating must have seemed like a new invention to the people around him because soon they began calling his bread-and-filling contraption a "sandwich."

Now, most of us don't get anything named after ourselves—unless it's a child. John Montagu not only got the sandwich named in his honor, but the Sandwich Islands also were named after him. Those islands, made famous by Captain Cook, are today known as Hawaii.

So much for the sandwich part of our story. As for the burger, we have to move across the English Channel. For hundreds of years, people around the Baltic Sea had enjoyed eating raw shredded beef. (Today, we call it "steak tartare.") Merchants carried the recipe for this meal to the town of Hamburg, Germany. For reasons known only to themselves, people began to call the dish hamburg-steak. It was served without bread on a plate, just like any other steak.

At the beginning of the twentieth century, German immigrants brought the hamburg-steak to America. Somewhere along the line, they started calling it "hamburger steak" and then just plain hamburger. Later the name got shortened even further, to "burger," as in Burger King.

In the United States, some people started frying the hamburger meat. This made the patty nice and firm, and it was only a matter of time before someone got the idea to use it as a sandwich filling. In 1904, the hamburger sandwich first got national attention at the St. Louis World's Fair, and it became a sensation.

During the 1930s, the hamburger was often called a "Wimpy," named after a character in the Popeye comic strip. Wimpy loved hamburgers as much as Popeye loved spinach. And he helped spread the popularity of the burger.

By the 1960s, to most people the hamburger was as American as apple pie. So when McDonald's began to open stores throughout Europe, many Europeans felt their countries were being invaded by an American invention. In reality, the hamburger was just coming home.

The 1904 St. Louis World's Fair where legend says the hamburger on a bun was first served.

How to Make Homemade Hamburgers

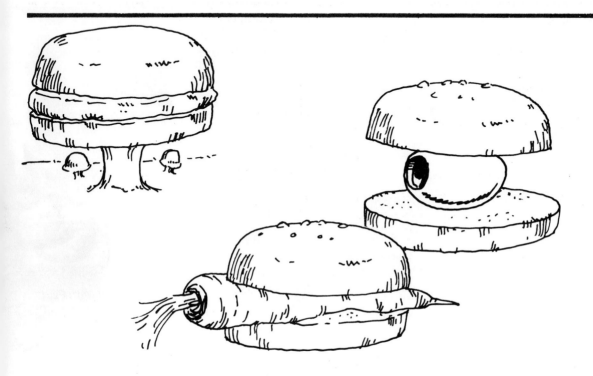

The McDonald Brothers were creative when it came to making hamburgers. But the real genius of sandwich-making has to be Dagwood, the husband in the comic strip *Blondie*.

Dagwood's philosophy about sandwiches is simple: anything goes. If you can be as free as that, you should have a lot of fun dreaming up your own hamburger variations. To get your imagination going, here is a basic burger recipe plus ten variations.

As for cooking the ground meat, there are a lot of theories on how to do it. At McDonald's, they fry the patties on a hot grill. Lots of people think the best taste comes from barbecuing the meat over hot coals. Recently, some people have said the healthiest way to do it is to broil the burgers. They should be rare, not over-done, and the fat should be allowed to drain off.

Basic Burger

1 pound ground beef
1 teaspoon salt
1 pinch of pepper
1 tablespoon chopped onion
1 tablespoon chopped parsley
1 egg (optional)

Mix ingredients together and shape into four or more patties.

Ten Ways to Make Hamburgers

Here are ten variations on the basic burger recipe:

Nut Burgers
¾ cup chopped walnuts, pecans or cashews

Olive Burgers
½ cup chopped black olives

Mushroom Burgers
¾ cup chopped, cooked mushrooms

Potato Burgers
¾ cup cooked mashed potatoes and 1 beaten egg

Carrot Burgers
1 grated carrot

Health Burgers
¾ cup uncooked oatmeal

Surprise Burgers
¾ cup of any cheese, grated

Swedish Burgers
1 tablespoon chopped fresh dill

Italian Burgers
½ cup grated Parmesan cheese and ½ teaspoon oregano

Mexican Burgers
½ cup chili sauce or 1 tablespoon chili powder

How to Be a Fast-Food Sleuth

It is easy as we just showed you on the previous page, to create your own taste treats at home. But what if you like the way fast-food places make their burgers, chickens, pizzas and so forth? Is there a way for you to prepare at home foods that taste like restaurant cooking?

Until recently, the answer for most people was "no." Fast-food restaurants guard their special recipes as if these sauces and batters and toppings were highly classified government secrets.

McDonald's, for instance, admits their Big Mac sauce starts with mayonnaise, but what it ends up with they won't reveal. (We know they won't because we asked them.)

Harlan Sanders, the Kentucky Fried Chicken "Colonel," explains that he used eleven spices found in most kitchens to create the flavor of his world-famous chicken. But exactly which eleven spices and in what proportions is for him to know and for the rest of us to find out.

Well, one of *us* has been trying to find out. Her name is Gloria Pitzer, and for the past several years she has been breaking the secret recipes of major fast-food chains across the country. Pitzer, who calls herself "the Junk Food Junkie," has tasted, sniffed, studied and analyzed everything from Taco Bell's tortillas to Tastee Freeze's frozen custard. She experimented for two years before coming up with her version of Arthur Treacher's fish batter. (It is made with pancake mix and club soda!)

This Sherlock Holmes of junk food shares her discoveries in two books plus a monthly newsletter. Her goal is to make it possible for people not only to enjoy eating junk food, but also to enjoy making it. She thinks it is creative to prepare junk food at home and a lot cheaper, too. (Actually, Pitzer does not believe that junk food is all that junky. She argues that most national fast-food places are clean. She also points out that doctors and nutrition experts disagree among themselves as to which foods—and how much of them—are dangerous to one's health.) You will find one of Gloria Pitzer's "discoveries" at the end of this spread.

Meanwhile, if you would like to try your own hand at breaking secret recipe codes, here's how to do it:

Let's say you want to try to duplicate a Big Mac in your own kitchen. First, you will need a sample Big Mac to study. You might order one at a McDonald's and examine it right there, but people at the next table will probably think you are a little strange. So we recommend that you do your work in your own kitchen.

The next step is *not* to take a bite. When you munch something that's all put together, it is almost impossible to identify the individual ingredients. So instead, you should take the Big Mac apart and list what you find:

top bun, toasted and coated with "secret sauce"
meat patty
pickle pieces
shredded lettuce
middle bun, coated with "secret sauce"
chopped onions
another meat patty
1 slice of cheese
more shredded lettuce
bottom bun, coated with "secret sauce"

If you are missing any of the above, go back and ask for another Big Mac.

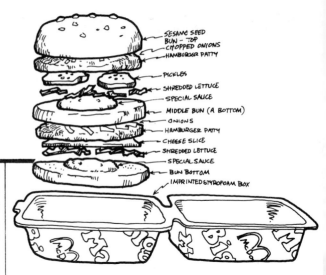

Now you are ready to analyze what you've got. Start with your eyes. Study the bun. Have you ever seen one like it at the supermarket or the bakery? Inspect the dressings—the onions, the pickles, the lettuce. If you are really serious, you might measure each element carefully. Use measuring spoons to calculate the amount of lettuce and onions, a measuring stick to size up the piece of cheese. Count the number of pickle pieces.

At this point bring your nose into operation. Sniff the pickles and the sauce. Do the aromas seem familiar? Can you place them?

Finally, you are ready to use that most delicate of food sleuthing tools—your tongue. Nibble a bit of the bun. Anything unusual about it? Chew a few of the sesame seeds. Try the cheese. Can you tell what kind? Is it Swiss or American or something even more exotic? Check out the pickles. Are they sweet or sour? And the meat. Is it tough or tender? Does it have much flavor? (By now its probably cold and dry—part of the price you pay for being a food code breaker.) Last but not least, sample the "secret sauce." Lick off a smidgen and keep it in your mouth. Is it tangy or sweet? Is it catsupy or mustardy?

The big question now is: can you create your own imitation Big Mac? The only way to answer that question is to try.

Gloria Pitzer's Junk Food Recipes

To avoid lawsuits, Gloria Pitzer uses made-up names to disguise the famous foods she is writing about. Here is her recipe for "Big Match Sauce."

BIG MATCH SAUCE
Mix together

1 cup Miracle Whip
1/3 cup Kraft Creamy French salad dressing
¼ cup undrained sweet pickle relish
1 tablespoon sugar
¼ tablespoon pepper
1 teaspoon minced onion.

Makes 2 cups, or enough for a dozen Big Match's.

This recipe was copyrighted and developed by Gloria Pitzer and taken from her cookbook, *Secret Restaurant Recipes Duplicated.* For further information on how to purchase Gloria Pitzer's recipes send her a self-addressed, stamped envelope:

GLORIA PITZER
Box 152
St. Clair, Michigan 48079

Reading List

If you want to know more about—and *do* more with—the subjects in *Made In America*, here is a list of starting points. Most are books. A few are magazines. One is a recording. A star (*) indicates a book that's easy to read.

Superman

All in Color for a Dime by Richard Lupoff and Don Thompson (Arlington House, New Rochelle, NY, 1970). A folksy history of the comics during the 1940s and 1950s.

The Great Comic Book Heroes by Jules Feiffer (Dial, New York, 1965). A large album-sized, full-color book with comments by one of America's great comic-strip writers. Feiffer's descriptions of what it was like to work in the comic-book industry during the 1940s are worth as much as the gallery of comic art he presents.

How To Make Old-Time Radio Plays by Ron Harris (Dead Pan Productions, 1111 Greenwood Ave., Palo Alto, CA 94301, 1976). This 60-minute audiocassette includes tips on scripting, acting, making sound effects and recording.

Superman: Serial to Cereal: The Saga of Movie and TV's Greatest Hero by Gary Grossman (Popular Library, New York, 1977). A behind-the-scenes account of how all the Superman movies and TV shows were made.

Teaching and Writing Popular Fiction: Horror, Adventure, Mystery and Romance in the American Classroom by Karen Hubert (Virgil Books, New York, 1976). Written for teachers, this is a book any would-be story writer will value.

Coca-Cola

*Collecting Things by Paul Villiard (Doubleday, New York, 1975). A guide to collecting dozens of different things including bottles, postal cards, barbed wire, stamps, toy soldiers and autographs.

*Peanuts, Popcorn, Ice Cream, Candy and Soda Pop and How They Began by Solveig Russell (Abingdon Press, Nashville, 1970). Lots of interesting facts told in an entertaining manner.

*Soda Pop: The History, Art and Memorabilia of Soft Drinks in America by Lawrence Dietz (Simon & Schuster, New York, 1973). This funny, fact-filled book focuses on Coca-Cola, but includes the stories of Pepsi, Hires, Royal Crown, Dr. Pepper, Moxie and other drinks. It's packed with historical photographs and art work.

Frisbee

Frisbee by Stancil Johnson (Workman, New York 1975). The most detailed history of the Frisbee, this book provides lots of throwing and catching tips, plus information on why a Frisbee soars, how to care for a Frisbee, and how to select a flying disc.

Frisbee Players' Handbook by Mark Danna and Dan Poynter (Parachuting Publications, Santa Barbara, CA, 1978) and Frisbee by the Masters by Charles Tips (Celestial Arts, Millbrae, CA, 1977). Two source books recommended to disc lovers by the International Frisbee Association.

Frisbee World Magazine (P.O. Box 970, San Gabriel, CA 91776, one-year subscription/6 issues $5.00). Covers skills, new games, personalities and news. Use same address for information on The International Frisbee Association.

*Kid's Dog: A Training Book by Richard Wolters (Doubleday, New York, 1978). If you want to do more than train your dog to catch a Frisbee, this should help. It tells how to select a puppy; when to start training; how to housebreak a dog; how to get a dog to sit, stay, come, be quiet, heel, speak, shake hands, beg, fetch, carry objects, roll over and jump barriers.

The New Games Book by the New Games Foundation (Doubleday, Garden City, NY, 1976). New and old games from around the world. The idea is to be active without getting hurt. The sixty games include Boffing, Ball Crawl, British Bulldog, New Volleyball, Eco-Ball, Hagoo and Water Slide.

Television

How Sweet It Was by Arthur Shulman and Roger Youman (Bonanza Books, New York, 1966). The history of television broadcasting from the early days of the 1940s to the 1960s, portrayed through 1435 photographs.

*The Incredible Television Machine by Lee Polk and Eda LeShan (Macmillan, New York, 1977). A general history of television with advice on how to control the tube rather than be controlled by it.

Monopoly

*Games You Can Build Yourself by Katharina Zechlin (Sterling, New York, 1975). Directions for building your own equipment for playing Go, Reversi, Cows and Leopards, and dozens of other games from around the world.

The Monopoly Book: Strategy and Tactics of the World's Most Popular Game by Maxine Brady (McKay, New York, 1974). Some commonsense observations on how to play the game without losing your (make-believe) shirt.

100 Ways to Win Monopoly Games: Skills, Strategies and Secrets the Experts Use by Jay Walker and Jeff Lehman (Dell, New York, 1975). How to raise instant cash, how to make your opponents pay off your debts for you, how to bargain, and other high-finance high jinks.

King Kong

Basic Titling and Animation. Available from local photo dealers or Eastman Kodak Company, Rochester, NY 14650). A how-to pamphlet written for the semi-professional with time, money and fancy equipment.

However, the serious amateur can easily adapt many processes to simpler set-ups.

Cinemagic. (Does not appear on a regular schedule. Write the editor at Box 125, Perry Hall, MD 21128 for information about the latest issue). A magazine put out by fans of special movie effects, especially in science-fiction, horror and monster movies. Features articles on how to do your own animation, make-up and the like—some simple, some quite complicated. Also runs pictures and stories of fans who have made their own movies.

*How To Make Your Own Movies by Harvey Weiss (Addison-Wesley, Reading, MA, 1973). Describes the basic techniques of filmmaking. Also deals with attitudes, interests and personal feelings that provide the basis for simple, effective movies. Full of suggestions and ideas.

Illustrated History of the Horror Film by Carlos Clarens (Putnam, New York, 1968). Plots, pictures and facts of all the major scary movies. Not recommended as bedtime reading unless you enjoy horror dreams.

Make Your Own Animated Movies by Yvonne Andersen (Little, Brown, Boston, MA, 1970). Based on the classes held at the Yellowball Workshop, where hundreds of kids learned filmmaking, this book covers clay animation, cut-out animation and drawing on film.

The Making of King Kong by Orville Goldner and George E. Turner (Hardback, Barnes, 1975; paperback, Ballantine, 1976). Collection of stories, photos and information about the making of the greatest monster movie of all time. It is the book on King Kong, not surprising since Orville Goldner was on the Kong technical staff and received screen credit for his work on the film. The book tells all about the producers, actors and the special effects.

Movie Magic: The Story of Special Effects in the Cinema by John Brosnan (St. Martin's Press, New

York, 1974). Details the secrets of the great special effects artists and how they made classic films like *War of the Worlds* and *The Incredible Shrinking Man.*

Movie Monsters: Monster Make-Up & Monster Shows to Put On by Alan Ormsby (Scholastic Book Services, New York, 1975). The first half of this book describes some of the classic monster faces and how they were created. The second half of the book presents recipes for monster-making—how to make "blood," scars, a dracula face, a mummy's hand and other things too terrible to mention.

Science Fiction in the Cinema by John Baxter (A. S. Barnes, New York, 1973). Overview of the fantastic visions of science-fiction filmmakers.

Starlog. (Published eight times a year by O'Quinn Studios Inc., 475 Park Ave. South, 8th floor suite, New York, NY 10016.) A professional magazine for fans of science-fiction movies, includes articles about the making of movies like *Star Wars.* Often tells how special effects are done.

Super-8 Filmaker Magazine (3161 Fillmore St., San Francisco, CA 94123; one-year subscription/8 issues $9.00). Articles about all kinds of filmmaking, including special effects, animation, travel and documentary, plus reviews of equipment and news about film festivals and contests.

The Technique of Film Animation by John Halas and Roger Manvell and **The Technique of Special Effects Cinematography** by Raymond Fielding (Hastings House, 10 East 40th Street, New York, NY 10016). Extremely detailed books aimed at the professional moviemaker. However, for someone who is really serious about finding out the "why" and "how," the principles are adaptable to amateur equipment. Books in this series are called the *Focal Library of Communication Techniques.*

Young Filmmakers by Rodger Larson and Ellen Meade (Dutton, New York, 1971). A thorough and helpful guide to filmmaking by two well-known film teachers.

Levi's

The Cowboys by the Editors of Time-Life Books with text by William Forbis (Time-Life Books, New York, 1973). An illustrated history that includes life on the range, cattle towns, clothing and survival techniques.

***Painting with Stitches: A Guide to Embroidery, Needlepoint, Crochet, and Macrame** by Vera Guild (Davis Publications, Worcester, MA, 1976). Beautiful pictures and simple directions make this a valuable manual of threaded art.

Rodeo: The Suicide Circuit by Fred Schnell (Rand, McNally, New York, 1971). Close-up on the thrills and spills of this dangerous sport.

McDonald's

Big Mac: The Unauthorized Story of McDonald's by Max Boas and Steve Chain (New American Library, New York, 1976). A fault-finding history of McDonald's that has lots of interesting facts and some interesting opinions, too.

Grinding It Out: The Making of McDonald's by Ray Kroc with Robert Anderson (Henry Regnery, Chicago, 1977). Ray Kroc's own story of how he built McDonald's into the most famous restaurant chain in the world.

New Hamburger and Hot Dog Cookbook by Mettja Roate (Arlington House, New York, 1975). Hundreds of recipes devoted to America's two most popular foods.

***Sandwichery: Recipes, Riddles & Funny Facts about Food** by Patricia and Talivaldsi Stubis (Parents' Magazine Press, New York, 1975). Serves up tips for making all kinds of sandwiches—roast beef, cottage cheese, triple decker, French hero and decorated "open face." You'll also find ideas for sandwich parties.

***You Are What You Eat: A Common Sense Guide to the Modern Diet** by Sara Gilbert (Macmillan, New York, 1977). Combines interesting food facts with sound advice on how to eat for health's sake.

Credits

We would like to thank the following for permission to reproduce the photographs and illustrations in this book:

Chapter 1
Page 5, The Cleveland Press; Page 5, drawing © 1961, DC Comics, Inc.; page 8 *top*, © 1938 Detective Comics, Inc., renewed © 1965 DC Comics, Inc., *bottom*, © 1940 McClure Newspaper Syndicate, renewed © 1968 DC Comics, Inc.; page 9 *top left*, © 1941 DC Comics, Inc., *middle* © 1948 Columbia Pictures Corp., renewed © 1976 DC Comics, Inc., *top right*, © 1951 DC Comics, Inc., courtesy The Bettman Archive, *bottom* © 1962 DC Comics, Inc.; page 11, © 1951 DC Comics, Inc.; page 22, © 1938 Detective Comics, Inc., renewed © 1965 DC Comics, Inc.; pages 6, 7, 12, 13, 14 *bottom*, 15 *left*, 16, 17, 18, 19, 20, 21, 24, 25, 37, Ron Harris Collection; page 10 *right*, page 18 *middle*, Murray Suid Collection; page 10 *left*, The Oster Company; page 14 *top*, reprinted by permission of the *Chicago Tribune, New York News* Syndicate, middle, AP Newsfeatures; page 15 *right*, page 23 *top*, © 1969, *bottom* © 1964, Marvel Comics Group, Division of Cadence Industries Corp., All Rights Reserved; page 27, The Viking Press; page 26, Bruce McIntyre; page 28, Simon & Schuster, Inc.; page 29, Henry Z. Walck, Inc.; page 35, DuMont Television Network.

Chapter 2
Pages 38, 41, 43, 44, 45, 46, 47, 48, 49, 50–51, The Coca-Cola Company; page 39, The Bettman Archive; page 41, Suthpen Studios; page 51 *right*, Real Thing Shop, 11650 Riverside Drive, North Hollywood, CA 91602.

Chapter 3
Pages 54, 55, 57, 60, 66, 63, Whamo Mfg. Co.; page 67, Ron Harris and Murray Suid; page 61, International Frisbee Association.

Chapter 4
Pages 68, 70, 71, 72, 73, courtesy of Mrs. Philo (Elma G.) Farnsworth; page 69, The Bettman Archive; page 76, San Francisco Fire Department; page 76 *lower left, middle right*, page 77 *lower right*, page 78 *middle right*, page 79 *lower right*, Columbia Broadcasting System; page 76 *lower right*, page 77 *upper left, upper right, middle left, bottom left*, page 78 *upper left, lower left, upper right, lower middle, lower right*, page 81 *upper right*, American Broadcasting Corporation; page 76 *upper right*, page 79 *upper left, upper right, lower left, middle left*, Public Broadcasting System; pages 80, 81, A. C. Nielsen Company; page 88, Mardex; page 89 *bottom*, Jack Ellis; page 89 *top*, page 94, photos courtesy of Sony Corporation of America; page 89 *middle*, "Video Weaving" electronic video artist—picture taken from screen of color television set—patterns made with Beck Direct Video Synthesizer—photo © 1977 by Stephen Beck, All Rights Reserved; page 90 *top left*, Stanford University Medical Center; page 90 *lower left*, page 91 *top*, VideoBrain Computer Co.; page 90 *right*, Warner Communications; page 91 *bottom*, Victoria Rouse; pages 92, 93, photos courtesy of NASA; pages 98–101, Dick Adler.

Chapter 5
Pages 103, 105, 106 *left*, 107 *right*, Ralph Anspach, Anti-Monopoly, Inc., d.b.a. Anspach Co., 201 D. Street, San Rafael, CA 94901; page 106 *right*, David Buckwalter; page 107 *top*, Daniel Layman; page 108, *lower left*, map and photo, Atlantic City PR Dept.; page 108, *middle* and *right*, page 109, Ed Davis; pages 112, 113, Toby Dills; pages 104, 110, 111, 115 *top left*, Ron Harris.

Chapter 6
Pages 117, 120, 121, 123 *top*, 124, 125 *right*, 126, 127, from the collection of Orville Goldner; pages 118, 122, 123 *right*, 124, The Bettman Archive.

Chapter 7
Pages 142–151, art page 152, courtesy of Levi Strauss & Co.; page 154, The Bettman Archive.

Chapter 8
Page 158, Richard J. McDonald; page 159, American Restaurant Magazine; page 161 *left*, Wide World Photos, *right*, Prince Castle Co.; page 163, McDonald's Corp.; pages 164, 165, photos courtesy of Armour Food Company; pages 166, 167, Keystone Foods Corp.; pages 168–171, Ron Harris; pages 176–177, The Bettman Archive.

Drawings throughout by Ron Harris, unless otherwise specified.

Index